leveraging your influence

Impacting College Students for Christ

Tim Elmore

foreword by Arliss Dickerson

LifeWay Press

Nashville, Tennessee

ISBN: 0-6330-9050-6

Dewey Decimal Classification Number: 303.3
Subject Heading: LEADERSHIP, CHURCH WORK WITH COLLEGE STUDENTS, COLLEGIATE MINISTRIES
Printed in the United States of America

Student Ministry Publishing
LifeWay Church Resources
One LifeWay Plaza
Nashville, Tennessee 37234-0175

We believe the Bible has God for its author; salvation for its end; and truth, without any mixture of error, for its matter and that all Scripture is totally true and trustworthy. The 2000 statement of The Baptist Faith and Message is our doctrinal guideline.

Unless otherwise noted, Scripture quotations marked HCSB have been taken from the *Holman Christian Standard Bible®* Copyright © 1999, 2000, 2002, 2004 by Holman Bible Publishers. Used by permission.

Order additional copies of this book
or other collegiate resources published by LifeWay by writing to Customer Service Center, MSN 113;
One LifeWay Plaza; Nashville, TN 37234-0113; by calling toll free (800) 458-2772;
by faxing (615) 251-5933; by ordering online at *www.lifeway.com;*
by e-mailing *customerservice@lifeway.com;* or by visiting a LifeWay Christian Store.

Art Herron, Editor In Chief
Rhonda Delph, Copy Editor
Charles Long, Graphic Designer
Cover Illustration, Garry Nichols

EQUIP
"Growing Leaders"
PO Box 1808
Duluth, GA 30096

If you are teaching this in a group study and would like teaching helps, you can find them electronically by going to *www.lifeway.com/download,* click on Student Ministry Publishing, then click on *Leveraging Your Influence.* Or you may contact LifeWay Christian Resources at 615-251-2783 for a free hard copy.

Contents

Acknowledgements

I entered this project with a bit of apprehension. I would not have felt good about it had it not been for the team that Student Ministry Publishing at LifeWay Christian Resources put together. With their help, we brainstormed the content you find in this resource. Thanks to the Baptist campus ministers, Baptist State Campus Directors, and seminary faculty who were part of this support team.

I also wish to thank Anne Alexander, my executive assistant, and Ben Ward, our one-year intern who labored with me to review and edit the chapters. It is definitely a team effort. They are strong where I am weak. In addition, I want to thank Noble Bowman, a campus minister who models the things I talk about in this book; and Holly Moore, my personal prayer partner who prays and fasts for me faithfully as I write. A special thanks goes to my wife, Pam, and children, Bethany and Jonathan, who allow me to "practice" my leadership on them. I love you. These folks have been the support team as I launched "Growing Leaders," a ministry to those who lead and equip students. You can check out our Web site at *www.growingleaders.com*.

Behind the scenes for the entire collegiate leadership series, of which this is the fourth book (designed specifically for collegiate leaders of college students), are Joe Graham, Loy Reed, Arliss Dickerson, Sam Fort, David James, Ken Owens, John Moore, Coby Penton, Chris Turner, and Jim Toole, without whose efforts this resource and the others in the series would not exist. To each of them I am indebted for their unique contributions.

This book was a special labor of love as it was the second book in the same year to be released by LifeWay. My special thanks to the editorial team at LifeWay for making this book a reality. Rhonda Delph, Charles Long, Judy Hewitt, and Art Herron, thanks for your patience, guidance, and the teamwork it took to produce this resource for collegiate leaders of students.

If you work with college students in leadership in any form, this book is for you. The seven sessions are intended to challenge you to be the model leader for those you lead in your collegiate program. My prayer is that it will strengthen you to do mighty things for Christ as He pours out His life to you.

—Dr. Tim Elmore

Foreword

By Arliss Dickerson, Baptist Collegiate Minister, Arkansas State University

Three years ago I attended a national conference on college ministry and I went to a seminar on developing student leaders. After the seminar was over I told a friend, "I just heard the best guy on developing student leaders I have ever heard." That new friend was Tim Elmore.

Tim brings the best of two worlds together. He not only knows what to do, but he knows *why* it works. Lots of people can give you ideas that have worked in certain situations but they might not work in yours. Tim understands the principle behind the activity and helps you know how it can fit into your ministry and lifestyle. Developing student leaders has long been a passion of mine. I believe that when you stop developing student leaders, you have begun the end of your ministry. *Leveraging Your Influence* is about developing yourself so you can better develop others.

Very often books written to help a college minister are aimed at those who have been in college ministry for about 20 minutes.

I am excited about this book because I think it is a great tool for the beginner or the campus minister who has seen it all. If you are brand new, it gives you some ideas of a place to start. But if you are not new at it, I think you will be surprised at the way it can help you step back from your ministry, evaluate it, and do some fine-tuning that will be very beneficial.

Some "how-to" books tell you how to imitate someone else and try to re-create their success. *Leveraging Your Influence* will help you evaluate and sharpen your own style. The self-assessment tools given are a strength of this book. You are the main tool your ministry has and Tim will help you make your main tool better.

Simply put, all of us want to do what we do better. I believe Tim Elmore is a friend who has done college ministry in a good way and even more importantly, can help you and me do it better.

You've Been Promoted!

"Then I heard the voice of the Lord saying: 'Whom shall I send? Who will go for Us?' I said, 'Here I am. Send me' "—Isaiah 6:8 (HCSB®)

"Our worst sins arise as a response to our innate fear that we are nobody."

Kent and Cheri are church planters in Croatia. They gave birth to a baby church where there was no church 10 years ago. Soon they will launch their second one.

Beau finished medical school at Columbia University and now practices medicine among the poor in New York.

Michael is a missionary aviator who works among an unreached people group in southern Asia. He can fly a plane and share Jesus as well as anyone I know.

Rob pastors in southern California and is raising up young leaders by the hundreds in his church and on the campuses nearby.

Kelly finished her degree in education and found a fertile mission field right in her hometown public high school, of all places.

> **Regardless of their courses of study, they saw themselves as ministers.**

What do these individuals have in common? They all got their start as students in our college ministry at Skyline Church in San Diego. Just over 400 of them answered a call to vocational ministry over the course of a decade. Thousands of university students made a choice to serve God, either in the marketplace or in church-related ministries. Regardless of their courses of study, they saw themselves as ministers. In retrospect, the most fulfilling task I undertook was equipping students for ministry. Today, almost anywhere I travel around the world, I find one or more of our former students ministering there.

This is a High Calling

Maybe I'm just narrow-minded, but I cannot think of a more rewarding way to spend my time than to invest in college students. I recognize it isn't vogue. I know I'm in the minority of those who feel this way. Many senior pastors believe it's a waste to hire a college minister because "students don't give back to the church." (I have heard them say this more than once). I disagree. Our students may not have had loads of money to give to the church, but they gave their time and energy at levels no older adult could muster. Their vision for ministry was mammoth, their passion unmatched. Some were ready to charge hell with a water pistol.

That's one of the many reasons why I love college students. It's why I continue working with them after 23 years. I believe the role of a campus minister or collegiate leader is a high calling. It is to be esteemed highly by those who fulfill that call. It should be valued greatly and taken seriously. It is more than a stepping stone until one can find a "real" ministry or one that pays better. That's nonsense. I know some who've served in collegiate ministry for 40 years and they wouldn't trade it for anything in the world. For them, it is a sacred trust.

Try This Out!

Take a moment and reflect on your past, specifically when you were between age 15 and 25. I'm guessing that you can remember specific individuals who helped to shape your life. Maybe it was for the better; maybe it was for the worse—but there were people of great influence. List some of those people here.

_____   _____

_____   _____

_____   _____

My speculation is, you had no trouble listing people who shaped your life as a young adult. Why do I say this?
- First, those years of your life are pivotal. We are so impressionable during those years. Some of the most lasting decisions are made during that time—our Master, our mate, and our mission. This is why it is so vital to serve as guides alongside college students today.
- Second, your desire to serve students likely was modeled by someone you wanted to emulate. This is why it is so vital to serve as models for college students.

Is It in the Bible?

I know what some of you are thinking. You're wondering if student ministry has any biblical basis. The answer is yes and no. Certainly, institutions of higher learning looked different for the ancient Hebrews than they look today. Samuel mentored a group of students for a prophetic ministry (1 Sam. 19:20). Elijah worked with a group of young men in his "school of the prophets." Their loyalty to him is evident as Elijah was taken away in 2 Kings 2. We learn in 2 Kings 4:1 that when one died he left his family in poverty. Evidently, the students didn't have much money. (Some things never change.) but they were able to help. A young man named Daniel and some other choice students were prepared to serve the king at a state school in Babylon (Dan. 1). Ashpenaz was hired to train them. (By the way, notice King Nebuchadnezzar's criteria for selecting these young student leaders).

Even in the New Testament students found educators and spiritual mentors to teach them. Young Saul of Tarsus found a teacher named Gamaliel with an outstanding reputation in the Sanhedrin (Acts 5:33-40). Gamaliel prepared Saul to be a passionate and educated leader (Acts 22:3). Without knowing it, Gamaliel equipped the greatest apostle ever to serve the church. During this time rabbis mentored young students in the Scriptures and in the traditions of the elders. Tutors were used as well. In my book, *The Greatest Mentors in the Bible*, I note 32 mentoring relationships in Scripture, many of whom were adults investing in younger students. Even Jesus selected 12 disciples who very likely were college-aged young men.

Hmmm. Maybe this idea of ministering to students isn't a new idea after all. Just maybe it's a God-thing. It's clear there is a divine emphasis on one generation preparing the next generation as far back as early Old Testament days. Could we conclude that discipling emerging young leaders on the campus is a high priority to God?

If I'm right, then this is a very high calling.

Some of the most lasting decisions are made during that time—our Master, our mate, and our mission.

Regardless of what you conclude about the biblical precedent for student ministry, there is a principle you must embrace about your calling today. In Isaiah 6:1-8 we read the passage in which Isaiah receives his call to serve. The experience included five stages:

- The Revelation of God (v. 1-2)—Isaiah has a face-to-face encounter with God.
- The Realization of God's Character (v. 3-4)—He hears the cry, "holy, holy, holy" and begins to understand who God really is.
- The Recognition of Isaiah's Own Sinfulness (v. 5)—He then is broken of his own self-life; he is empty and he knows it.
- The Renewal of Isaiah's Perspective (v. 6-7)—Next, the angel touches his lips, which cleanses and renews his perspective.
- The Response of Isaiah's Lifestyle (v. 8)—Finally, when God calls for a leader, Isaiah steps forward and volunteers.

Notice something significant about Isaiah's calling. God prepared him to respond to a need and took him through a process to get him ready. When God asked, "Whom shall I send? Who will go for Us?" Isaiah didn't hear anyone call his name specifically. It was a general call to which anyone could have responded. Isaiah responded because of these factors present in his life:

- Ability—God prepared Isaiah with the relevant ability to minister to Israel.
- Opportunity—God placed in front of Isaiah an opportunity that fit his sphere of influence.
- Desire—God placed in Isaiah a heart for the people to whom he would minister.

God prepared Isaiah to respond to a need. What about you on your campus? Is God preparing you?

Consider for a moment your calling. I believe God will often call us in the same way. No doubt, some may hear an audible voice telling them where to serve; others may sense an inward confirmation about a specific place of ministry. Many, however, will simply find the same three factors that Isaiah experienced when it comes to college ministry: ability, opportunity, and willingness. Let me ask you in a straightforward fashion:

Has God prepared you with a relevant ability to connect with college students?
Has God laid in front of you an opportunity to influence a college campus?
Has God given you a heart for college students that compels you to go?

"If God calls you to be a missionary, don't stoop to be a king." I love that statement. Let me amend it now, for our purposes. If God calls you to work with college students, don't stoop to do anything else. For some it may be full-time, some as volunteers, others as pastors of churches near universities. Wherever and whoever you are, don't forget your calling!

Why Do I Work with College Students?

I began working with college students in 1979 while I was working on my theology degree. I oversaw the junior high, senior high, and collegians at a little church of 150 people. During those four years at the church, college students got under my skin. While I enjoyed my ministry to adults, parents, and even senior adults in the church, I felt compelled to invest time in those young adults.

Along the way, I drew a conclusion: Equipping young adults is strategic to the church and to God's kingdom. The ones I was privileged to lead were so impressionable. They were so hungry to grow spiritually and be discipled. They wanted to have fun, yet they were determined to make a difference in the world. Welcome to the world of collegians! We who work with them get the chance to mold the next generation of laborers to enter the harvest fields.

That's only the beginning, however. There are other important reasons why I choose to minister to university students. Let me share with you a few of those reasons.

1. Because the Need is So Great.

There are almost 4,000 colleges in the U.S. today. Roughly 16,000,000 students are enrolled on those campuses.[1] The vast majority of the campuses have a weak Christian presence on them, if there is any at all. The largest college ministry, Baptist Collegiate Ministries, is on about one-fourth of the schools. There is one campus worker per 1,000 students.[2] Campus ministers who work with Campus Crusade for Christ, Navigators, Chi Alpha, Wesley Foundation, InterVarsity, and others are seen as missionaries. And they are. While there is a deep spiritual hunger among the Millennial generation, a huge percentage of them are not looking to the church for spiritual answers. Each year seems to mark an all-time high in the number of incoming freshman professing "no religious preference."[3] They pray, but most are not Christian, nor do they attend church.

Is it any wonder why? Most churches have no college ministry. Pastor Dan Bauman, a colleague from my days in San Diego, took a sabbatical one year to travel and see what was happening among the churches in America. He drew several conclusions. One of them was simply that there's a dearth of college ministry going on. Even churches located next to college campuses often feel they don't need a staff member to minister exclusively to students. The typical response is: "They're right across the street. They can find their way over to the church." Even churches that sponsor college ministries invest relatively little funds in it. Again, students are perceived as consumers who don't give back. Money is invested in high schoolers because of their parents, and is invested in young marrieds because they're adults who finally have something to put in the offering plate. College students are caught in between. Only churches that see beyond their local interests and begin to think "kingdom" pursue collegians.

What's more, college life often pulls students away from their involvement in the church and their relationship with Jesus Christ. During the 1920s Frank Leavell saw this problem clearly as he worked with Baptist teens. He watched high school students leave home for college as committed Christians, faithful to the church and passionate for God. But when those same students returned home from college, it was all too rare to find them indifferent and sometimes even hostile. Their spiritual development had not kept pace with intellectual and social horizons that were expanding under the college experience. Frank realized he was losing all he had invested into them in the youth programs. He knew something had to be done and his work with the BYPU had prepared him for it. He became the first national secretary for the Baptist Student Unions. He designed a plan to meet the spiritual needs of the college campus.

And the need continues to this day. The spiritual climate at colleges is often cold. Safe relationships are sought at fraternities, sororities, or at parties. University staff and faculty frequently fail to step in to really get to know students. William Willimon wrote an article entitled, "Reaching and Teaching the Abandoned Generation." He tells of how he begged Duke University staff to get involved with their students' problems. One dean responded, "But what can we do? After all, we are not their parents."[4]

2. Because Universities are Bootcamps for Leaders.

Consider this: tomorrow's leaders are on some college campus today. Over 70% of the international leaders in government and business will do some of their study in the U.S.[5] Our universities are incubators for young leaders who will direct our churches, our businesses, and our government. I realize this sounds trite, but we have the opportunity to shape them now.

While it's true that students may not learn healthy, effective leadership in the classroom, the years they spend at college are their preparation—good or bad—to lead in the future. In fact, leadership was the very purpose of college in America. Don Shockley writes, "In founding Harvard, the first institution of higher learning…the colonists were acting on their hope of creating an exemplary society, a new order in which the intention of God for human life will prevail. Their mission was to train what might be thought of as morally intelligent leadership for the whole community, not just for the church."[6]

If God calls you to be a missionary, don't stoop to be a king.

I do not argue that universities are the only place young leaders are formed. Some leaders never go to college and are prepared in the school of "hard knocks." I believe most American leaders can trace some leadership preparation to their college experience. Many church leaders—pastors and laypeople—can point to leadership preparation in a Baptist Student Union, Bible study, or another campus ministry. Ready or not, they are learning leadership from you. When Mike Woodruff, founder of the Ivy Jungle Network, surveyed campus ministers, he discovered that the number-one challenge facing those workers was leadership development.

I believe we must be intentional about equipping students to lead. The Kellogg Foundation sponsored a study on how well universities are equipping them to be leaders. Dr. Helen and Alexander Astin (UCLA) led the task force, which drew some interesting conclusions. They reported, "The general education programs in most institutions are still notably lacking in requirements or other content that focuses on leadership."

The scholars concluded, "It is not enough to turn out graduates who have mastered knowledge in traditional disciplinary fields. Higher education institutions need to help students develop the personal qualities and abilities that are crucial to effective leadership...leadership is no longer the province of the few, the privileged, or even the ambitious...it is for everyone. Anyone, regardless of formal position, can be a leader."[7]

3. Because This is the Season Students Make Major Life Decisions.

During the years after high school but before marriage and mortgages, most young adults lay the track they'll follow for the rest of their lives. Again, the college years are when they make decisions about their Master, their mate, and their mission. Many of the mission movements of the last 200 years began with college students who chose to give up their pursuit of a high-paying job, and go to a foreign field as a missionary. They made radical decisions that would have been difficult to make if they had settled down with a spouse, kids, and house payment.

The U.S. Department of Labor reported that the average American makes seven major decisions in his/her adult life. Five of the seven are made (or at least begun) in college.[8] Think about the choices you made as a university student, and how it affected where you are today. For most, decisions about relationships, location, religion, lifestyle preferences, and vocation are made in college. The only two that aren't made in the young-adult years are retirement and investments. This is why it is so crucial to create environments for students to experiment with ministry opportunities and with leadership roles.

A student at San Diego State University, Julie visited my office every month to talk about her "life mission." This was not uncommon. Each year I took my students through an exercise to help them think through their purpose in life. In one of our meetings, Julie was anguishing over whether to change majors, and what direction she should take her junior year. I finally asked her, "Julie, what do you see God doing in your life on a regular basis? Are there any patterns?"

She thought for a moment, then nonchalantly responded, "Well, every summer I go down to Mexico on a short-term mission trip." She paused. "Then, of course, on spring break I go to Mexico again for our Mexicali outreach. I usually go in December again to help translate Spanish in Tijuana. And I go in the fall each year to help with the orphanage we sponsor."

We both smiled. I suggested that maybe God was placing the direction for her life right in front of her, and she had made the issue too complex and academic. I asked her if she'd ever considered serving as a missionary in Mexico. When she told me she could never be a leader, I replied: "What do you think you're doing each time you go there?" She smiled again. To make a long story short, Julie is now serving as a missionary in Mexico.

Julie is not alone. Many young adults made this kind of decision throughout history. They are not waiting until mid-life to make a difference. Let me remind you of a few...

King Josiah was eight years old when he became king of Judah. By the time he was a teenager, he had matured into a solid leader, and by age 20, he led a major spiritual reform.

As a college student, **John Wesley** started his "holy club" with his brother Charles. He was passionate about reforming a spiritually dead Anglican church. By the time he was 17 he founded the organization that later became the Methodist denomination.

Joan of Arc was a young lady cut from the same cloth. She knew her life mission when she was 15 years old. She led an army of 3,000 French knights to victory in the Battle of Orleans when she was only 17 years old.

Charles Spurgeon was a well-known pulpit orator when he was just 16 years old. He was only 21 when he became pastor of the Metropolitan Tabernacle in London, where he spoke to crowds of 10,000 people.

George Williams was 23 when he founded the Young Men's Christian Association, or the YMCA. This organization was a major source of spiritual revitalization among college students in the middle part of the 19th century.

Louis Braille went blind as a young boy, and soon was sent off to a school for the blind. His greatest frustration was that he couldn't read great books due to his blindness. So, as a teenager, he created a system of raised dots, enabling blind people to read. It was superior to any method at the time. His system, named after him, is in common use today.

How about **Albert Einstein?** Although he flunked math twice in school, it was because he was ahead of his time. He wrote his first paper on the theory of relativity at age 16.

And don't forget the story of **Bill Gates**. His mom bought some used electronic equipment at a garage sale for her "geek" son. He was only a teenager at the time. By the time he was 19, he formed Microsoft with his friend, Paul Allen.

4. Because This Generation is Primed to Make a Difference.

The way I see it, many of us have a classic love/hate relationship with college students. We love their energy, their creativity, their carefree pursuit of new possibilities, their sense of hope. But we hate their defiance, their unpredictability, their ease with change, and their propensity to challenge what everyone holds dear. The fact is, every generation of collegians shares these qualities. However, the Millennial generation—students born between 1984 and 2002, are different than their predecessors in other ways. (The older we get, the more this is clear!) Think about today's college student:

They were the first infants to ride in a mini-van with the sign: baby on board.
They grew up with Fox as a network.
They have always been able to choose long-distance carriers.
John Lennon and John Belushi have always been dead.
They have always been able to find weather reports on TV 24-hours-a-day.
George Foreman has always sold grills.
They never knew Madonna when she was "like a virgin."
They grew up with Microsoft, Nutrasweet, CDs, and DVDs.
The term *adult* has come to mean *dirty*.
They have spent more than half their lives with Bart Simpson.
They have never feared a nuclear war.
President Kennedy's assassination is as significant to them as Lincoln's.
There have always been women on the Supreme Court and traveling in space.
They have probably never dialed a phone.
The term "you sound like a broken record" must be explained.

> The way I see it, most of us have a classic love/hate relationship with college students.

Millennials
rely on family
to be a sanctuary
from the troubles
of the world
in which they live.

It is important to get a big-picture perspective on this Millennial generation. On the following page I've provided a chart that summarizes the last five generations of Americans. For the first time, five generations have been alive at the same time. Although I am generalizing here, I want you to note the changes in mindset and how they react to the previous generation.

LEADERSHIP ISSUE	SENIORS	BUILDERS	BOOMERS	BUSTERS	MILLENNIALS
Era they were born in	1900-1928	1929-1945	1946-1964	1965-1983	1984-2001
Life paradigm	Manifest destiny	Be grateful you have a job	You owe me	Relate to me	Life is a cafeteria
Attitude to authority	Respect them	Endure them	Replace them	Ignore them	Choose them
Role of relationships	Long-term	Significant	Limited: useful	Central, caring	Global
Value systems	Traditional	Conservative	Self-based	Media	Shop around
Role of career	Loyalty	Means for living	Central focus	Irritant	Place to serve
Schedules	Responsible	Mellow	Frantic	Aimless	Volatile
Technology	What's that?	Hope to outlive it	Master it	Enjoy it	Employ it
Market	Commodities	Goods	Services	Experiences	Transformations
View of future	Uncertain	Seek to stabilize	Create it	Hopeless	Optimistic

Summary of the Millennial Generation

Neil Howe and William Strauss wrote a definitive book on this new generation entitled, *Millennials Rising*.[9] Their conclusions, coupled with surveys I have taken with 3,000 students over the last two years, can be summarized with the following words.

1. *They feel special.*—Movies, government focus, and parents have all contributed to making this generation of students believe they are vital to our future. *USA Weekend* polled 272,400 teenagers. When asked, "In general, how do you feel about yourself?" 93% responded either "really good" or "kind of good." Only 6% said "not very good" and just 1% said "bad."[10]

2. *They love family.*—Millennials rely on family to be a sanctuary from the troubles of the world in which they live. Even students who came from a broken family will attempt to create a family in some other way (usually either on campus or in the church). The explosion of child-safety rules and devices has sheltered many of them, and parents have led the way. When asked, "Who are your heroes?" students did not list athletes for the first time in 25 years. Their number-one answer was Mom and Dad. Their number-two answer was Grandma and Grandpa.

3. *They are confident.*—Millennials believe they can make a difference. With high levels of trust and connection to each other, they often boast about their generation's power and potential. They are self-reliant and are comfortable acting on what they've been taught by adults. For the first time in 25 years, today's young adults believe the world can and will get better.

4. *They are mediavores.*—This generation is addicted to media—TV, computers, video games, CD players, DVD players, the Internet, music, and movies. It is not uncommon for them to be simultaneously doing homework, listening to a CD, watching television, and communicating with someone online. They give new definition to the term *multi-tasking*. There is an unfortunate side to this addiction. A Christian college official recently told me that 60% of their male students were watching pornography on the Internet. They added that the problem with their women was chat rooms. Both were patterns that held their minds hostage.

5. *They are team-oriented.*—Think about it. They grew up with Barney the Dinosaur, played soccer, learned in groups at school, and often wore school uniforms. Unlike previous generations, community accomplishment is more important than individual accomplishment. One man contrasted them from their parent's generation: "While Boomers may be bowling alone, Millennials are playing soccer in teams." They are developing solid team instincts and tight peer bonds. Many even date in groups! Community is the word to describe their lifestyles.

6. *They are global.*—This generation, probably the most mobile group ever, promises to build relationships with people all over the world. They plan to travel worldwide just as they already have on the Internet. Many will develop friends with people around the world through the Internet without ever meeting them in person. Short-term mission trips are up—over half of the missionary force overseas is composed of short-term workers.

7. *They are pressured.*—They have been pushed to study hard, avoid personal risks, and take advantage of the opportunities their family has afforded them. Schedules are tight for parents and students, so they have grown up with the stress of school, soccer leagues, Scouts, youth group, and increased homework. I recently saw a cartoon that depicted two female students walking off the practice field. One said to the other: "You have 10 minutes between soccer practice and piano lessons? What are you gonna do with all that free time?"

8. *They are harmonious.*—For the first time in decades, this is a generation that is cooperative and conventional. They take pride in their behavior and are more comfortable with traditional values than any generation in memory. They believe the past two generations were too selfish. When an interviewer asked a 17-year-old, "How is your generation going to rebel?" he replied, "The best way for me to rebel is to dress formally all the time, respect my elders, love my country, and drive a used Toyota instead of the prerequisite SUV."[11]

9. *They are generous.*—The Millennials not only enjoy accomplishment, they enjoy giving away their resources and serving communities. One campus reported that the average freshman had $87 of discretionary income per week to spend. And they do. Around 50% of college students are active in community service today. Many schools even give credit for extracurricular activities that serve others in the community. During one spring-break period, college students gave over $8,000,000 to Habitat for Humanity. This did not include the cost of their time. They want to help others and leave the world a better place.

10. *They are optimistic achievers.*—They may be the best-educated, best-behaved adults in the nation's history. Some have described them as the builder generation with technology. Unlike Gen Xers, they are full of hope instead of being pessimistic. Their optimism drives their behavior, causing them to over-commit and become involved in too many calendar-options available to them.

In any case, we have an opportunity to work with this Millennial generation for the next 20 years. As you work with them in your collegiate program, I believe:
- We must capitalize on our time to mentor them.
- We must give them realistic goals and expectations.
- We must help them make longer-term commitments.
- We must challenge them to limit their activities and do one or two things well, instead of 17 things with mediocrity.
- We must help them to see that discipleship is a process not an event, and that it's not always pleasurable.

If we're successful, we may see this generation finish the task of world evangelism.

5. Because Divine Movements Often Begin with College-Aged People.
One of the most compelling reasons to work with collegians is history. Have you taken the time to notice how often God uses college-aged young people to begin movements? It's uncanny. Clarence Shedd, in his book *Two Centuries of Student Movements,* writes: "The whole history of the Christian church tends to show the clearest vision (for changing the world) had generally come from students, who, taking seriously Jesus' way of life and His attitude toward God and man, had been restless until in some effective way they were enabled to share their views with every living human being."[12]

The young adults we meet with each week are the ones God may look to for radical obedience in a whole new direction.

Today it is time for another movement. Are your students ready? Are you?

The young adults we meet with each week are the ones God may look to for radical obedience in a whole new direction. They may be the catalysts. Are you a skeptic? Consider this:

- Jesus walked the earth 2000 years ago. While He took the time to preach, heal, and meet needs, He invested the majority of His time in 12 men. It's my belief they were young adults. Most were in their 20s. Because the apostle John lived until A.D. 95, it's possible that he was only in his late teens when Jesus called him to follow. Jesus knew these young men would be "new wineskins" who were ready for new wine.

- John and Charles Wesley, along with their friend George Whitfield, assembled at Oxford University for the purpose of prayer and personal accountability. They longed to live holy lives, but knew it would not come by merely attending church services. These three men each multiplied their ministries in thousands of converts. Wesley went on to establish similar accountability groups, called "class meetings," for his disciples. They became the charter members of the Methodist church.

- Samuel Mills was born in 1783. He enrolled at Williams College and began to meet with other students for prayer. One afternoon, the students got caught in a rainstorm and sought refuge under a haystack. The focus of their prayer time that day was foreign missions. Their haystack meeting became a worship service that birthed the American Protestant missionary movement. Mills organized them into the "Society of Brethren." Four years later, six of those haystack students sailed to Calcutta as missionaries.[13]

- Another infamous group was called The Cambridge Seven. In the 1860s, seven college students at Cambridge University in England decided to meet together to pray and discuss the needs of the world around them. They were especially burdened for China. From those seven students came another movement of workers that impacted China by the end of the 19th century. Again, this was a collegiate movement. There is little evidence of any adult leadership.

- At the end of the 19th century, Christians felt the same urgency we did at the close of the 20th century. They wanted to finish the task of reaching the world for Christ. Men such as John Mott and Dwight Moody traveled to college campuses compelling students to surrender their lives to the cause of the Great Commission. What emerged was the Student Volunteer Movement. Before it was over, 100,000 students stood up to be part of reaching the world by giving, praying, or going overseas. More than 30,000 actually went to a foreign field—the largest missions mobilization up to that point. Many of those who moved overseas packed all of their belongings in pine boxes. They knew they would likely die early, and this box would serve as their casket.[14]

- No one is better known for his role in the Welsh revival than a young student named Evan Roberts. This awakening occurred in 1904-1905, when Evan left his work mining coal to return to Loughor, his hometown, to share the gospel with people there. Over a series of weeks, and probably to the surprise of the somewhat timid coal miner, those awakened by the Spirit grew from an initial handful to virtually tens of thousands.[15]

- George Verwer was an 18-year-old Moody Bible Institute student when God spoke to him about the Great Commission. He took a team of other students to Mexico to serve, while enabling his friends to catch a vision for the world. This began the ministry we call Operation Mobilization. Hundreds of thousands of people have been impacted by the tens of thousands of O.M. missionaries. It all began with a student.

In fact, each of these movements began with students. Today it is time for another movement. Are your students ready? Are you?

Assessment

What are your earliest memories of God's call on your life? Jot down one or two.

Are you pursuing that call? (Check all that apply. You may want to talk with a pastor or mentor about your answers.)

       ❑ Yes ❑ No ❑ Not exactly   ❑ I'm on the pilgrimage to get it done.
       ❑ I have given up the call.   ❑ I really need help in understanding the call.

What is your level of passion for student ministry, on a scale of 1 to 10 and 10 being the highest? Why did you mark it where you did?

1   CONTINUUM   10

What are the compelling reasons you work with students? Jot down three or four reasons.

If you could change anything about your ministry to students, what would it be? We've allotted space for you to jot down several things.

Further Reading

When God Walked on Campus, Michael Gleason, Joshua Press, 2002
Millennials Rising, Neil Howe and William Strauss, Knopf Publishing, 2000
Two Centuries of Student Christian Movements, Clarence Shedd, Association Press, 1934
Campus Ministry—The Church Beyond Itself, Don Shockley, Westminster/John Knox Press, 1989
Leadership Insights, Steve Moore, Topflight Leadership, 2002
Nurturing the Leader Within Your Child, Tim Elmore, Thomas Nelson Publishers, 2001

Traveling on the Inside

THE INWARD LIFE OF A CAMPUS MINISTER

"Guard your heart above all else, for it is the source of life."
—Proverbs 4:23 (HCSB®)

"When I lay down the reins of this administration, I want to have one friend left. And that friend is inside myself."—Abraham Lincoln

Did you see the 2003 movie, *Catch Me If You Can?* Based on the life of Frank Abagnale, Jr., it told the true story of a young man who had a wild and crazy life as a doctor, an airline pilot, a surgeon, and an attorney, among other things. The irony behind the story is, he wasn't any of those in reality. He deserved an academy award for his portrayal of these professions. He was an intentional fake...a fraud...a pretender. Frank had dropped out of high school and began to con his way through life. It began early in his childhood when he discovered his uncanny talent to convince people that he was "somebody" through his sheer confidence and acting ability. People believed him and paid him handsomely for his services, but it was all a show. His lifestyle eventually caught up with him. He was always looking over his shoulder as the FBI stalked him. He was constantly making up lies to cover himself. The weight of having to fake it became too heavy. Eventually, he got caught and served time in prison.

When I read the book on Frank's life, I was intrigued, to say the least. But I was also gripped by how his story reflected mine as a minister. It's just an analogy, but as I talk with other men and women in ministry, many confess the same feelings. We start well, but eventually we swerve to one side, and lose our first love. Our lives get busy and we begin to fake our Christian lives, spiritual disciplines, and eventually ministries. Soon we pretend as a "lifestyle," and use up most of our energy looking over our shoulders to make sure we don't get caught. Our pet sins become regular, but we hide them. We preach on evangelism, but don't really do it. We pretend to have a great prayer life. We say all the right words to our students, because we want them to stay involved. It's all a performance. Unfortunately, this is a common story.

I recently spoke to a campus minister who confided to me: "Tim, I feel like such a fake. I don't really know what I'm doing here, and what I do know to do, I fail to do. If these students knew who I really was, they wouldn't keep coming."

Another told me how he feels he needs to keep secrets from his wife. "She would lose all respect for me as a minister if I told her what I've thought and done." Sometimes our secrets aren't that bad, but they're just as real. We know what we ought to accomplish, but we don't measure up. We start comparing ourselves to our colleagues. We look in the mirror and don't see a holy man or woman who models the Christian life very well. We see imperfections. We silently conclude: *If people knew who I really am, they wouldn't follow me.*

> We start well, but eventually we swerve to one side, and lose our first love.

The Art of Self-Leadership

Last year I read an article by Bill Hybels, pastor of Willow Creek Community Church. He suggests that great leaders don't merely lead those below them on the flow chart. Great leaders lead *up* (their superiors), *across,* (their colleagues), *down* (their subordinates) and, most of all, they lead *within* (themselves). Great leaders practice the art of self-leadership.[1] Your toughest leadership challenge will almost always be yourself.

I believe the battle with feeling like a fake can be resolved if we understand this truth. If we feel like a pretender, it's because we're not living the life we profess. We haven't led ourselves well. We must first come to grips with the grace of God—we really don't measure up, but His grace is sufficient for any circumstance we face. Then we must recognize how important it is to lead ourselves before we try to lead anyone else. If we'll concentrate on self-leadership before we try to lead others, we will naturally ripple into the other arenas of our lives.

Try This Out!

Think about the people you deeply respect—the ones you'd follow anywhere. Then write down the qualities that make them so influential or that make you respect them.

Here's my guess: The qualities you listed probably had more to do with self-leadership than they did with outward talents or mechanics. I tend to respect and follow others because of how they lead their own lives, more than some technique or skill they've mastered. Leadership doesn't begin when we become a great speaker or a popular campus minister. For me, it began when I decided I would lead *me* well, then I would try to lead others. What I discovered was, when I led *myself* well, *others* came to me for leadership.

My Problem

Prior to this decision, I placed far too much emphasis on my gifts and my up-front ministry. I consistently worked on my speaking skills, the study of group dynamics, and how to launch an attractive program. I was getting pretty good at those things, until one day I got a wake-up call in a most unlikely place. It was my home. My wife and I bought our first home in San Diego. Like in many subdivisions, the contractors built the house, and also put sod in the front lawn. However, they did nothing with the backyard. That was up to the homeowner.

Because I was so busy with my ministry, I did nothing with that back lawn for more than two years. It was just dirt clods and tumbleweeds. Thankfully, the builders put a big six-foot-high fence around it so no one could see it! One day, as I stood at our sliding-glass door, peering out at the dirt and thinking I really ought to do something back there, God got my attention. He impressed this thought: *Tim, you have treated your life like you have treated your yard.*

Recognizing the Lord was trying to say something to me, I prayed and asked what He meant by that statement. Suddenly, it all became clear to me. It was as though God said to me: "The public side of your life, like your front lawn, looks great. Just like that green sod and those palm trees growing in your front lawn, you have a public ministry that makes everyone think your life is totally together. The backyard, however, is like the private side of your life." Because no one could see it, I gave it little attention. And it was dirt. My spiritual disciplines were poor. My time alone with God was irregular and based on how busy I was that day. My prayer time was a grocery list, not an intimate conversation with my Father in heaven. I preached well, but it was a performance. I was an empty shell. That day, I made a decision I would do what was necessary to lead myself well.

...we must recognize how important it is for us to lead ourselves before we try to lead others...

When I led myself well, others came to me for leadership.

Is It in the Bible?

In 1 Samuel 30, David was a young leader, preparing to become king of Israel. He was learning to lead his troops in battle, but he was still green. One terrible day, he and his men returned home from fighting yet another enemy, only to find some soldiers had attacked and destroyed their campsite, taken the women and children, and burned their belongings.

That's not all. David's soldiers were hungry, angry, lonely, and tired. This was not a good day for things to go bad. They were mad at God. Now they were anxious about their families. They were at the end of their ropes. One group began to spread word that they'd had it with David's leadership. They concluded it was David's fault and decided to stone him to death.

In this crisis, David's leadership was severely tested. Suddenly, he had to decide who needed leadership the most. His soldiers? The officers? The faction that rose up against him?

His answer? None of the above. In this critical moment, he realized a foundational truth: he had to lead himself before he could lead anyone else. Unless he was centered internally he had nothing to offer his team. David "found courage in the LORD his God" (1 Sam. 30:6). Only then did he lead his team to rescue their families and what was left of their belongings. David understood the importance of self-leadership. Although it isn't spoken about much, this is where it all begins. If you're weary, your confidence sagging, and your commitment weak, how will you lead your people anywhere?

> Strong character is simply leading yourself well.

Defining Character

What we are talking about here is character—godly, strong character. I have said for years that strong character is simply leading yourself well. Every leader must build an infrastructure of strong character and healthy relationships if they're going to lead well for a lifetime. At a county fair a few years ago, a man encountered a little girl with a huge mass of cotton candy on a paper cone. He asked, "How can a little girl like you eat all that cotton candy?"

"Well, Mister," she answered. "I'm really much bigger on the inside than I am on the outside."

That's exactly the kind of campus ministers God wants to raise up—those whose substance is bigger than their image. Good character is to be praised more than outstanding talent. To some extent, most talents are a gift. Good character, by contrast, is not given to us. We must build it, piece by piece, through thought, choice, and action.

Here is what I think a leader's character consists of: Character is the sum total of our personal identity, self-discipline, emotional security, and core values.

Personal Identity

> Character is the sum total of our personal identity, self-discipline, emotional security, and core values.

I believe strong character begins by settling the issue of personal identity. A strong moral compass comes from one who has determined who they are in Christ. We often think self-esteem is an issue for junior high school students. Not true. In a poll of pastors, the Barna Research Group and the Fuller Church Growth Institute came up with some startling statistics:
- 70% surveyed said their self-image is lower now than when they entered the ministry.
- 90% reported they feel inadequate for the tasks in front of them.
- 75% responded anonymously that they feel intimidated by the lay leaders or staff with whom they work.
- 65% said they have seriously considered quitting the ministry within the last two months.[2]

If we were able to conduct a poll reflecting the same issues among those who work with college students, what would the statistics look like? How would your stats look?

Perhaps this is why Dee Hock, business leader/author for over 20 years, challenges leaders to calculate how much time and energy they invest in each category of their leadership: leading people beneath them, leading peers, leading people above them, and leading themselves. His assessment is worth sharing.

He recommends we invest 50% of our leadership energy into the task of leading ourselves; the remaining 50% should be divided into leading down, leading up, and leading laterally—interesting insight into how we divide our time and energy. As a campus minister, leading down, leading up, and leading laterally may mean working with students, administration/faculty, and with our professional peers in churches and with pastors.

For us, this means we spend a chunk of our time ensuring our relationship with Jesus is intimate and vital. Perhaps it means we take a day alone with God once a quarter, just to regain perspective and direction. My practice is to get a D.A.W.G. (Day Alone With God) two to four times a year. I get away from people and get my bearings, just as Jesus did in Mark 1:35-38.

Perhaps Jesus was talking about self-leadership when He said: "A good tree doesn't produce bad fruit, nor again does a bad tree produce good fruit. A good man produces good out of the good storeroom of his heart, and an evil man produces evil out of the evil storeroom" (Luke 6:43,45). Leadership starts from within. It's *being* before *doing*. The hands only do what is in the heart.

When we have settled who we are in Christ, we don't have to play games or get defensive about our reputation. We don't feel compelled to project our self worth to others, or to prove something. We are free to be us. We can live from our position in Christ instead of our experience. We have nothing to prove, nothing to lose, and nothing to hide. Our authority is drawn from being "new creatures in Christ," not from our title or position. I learned this in 1979, the year before I became a student pastor. I was struggling with unhealthy self-esteem when I began a study of the New Testament passages that say anything about who I am "in Christ, in Him, or with Him." I highlighted these, and wrote them down. I drew a diagram of the crucial ones, and hung it on my bathroom mirror for a year. It looked something like this:

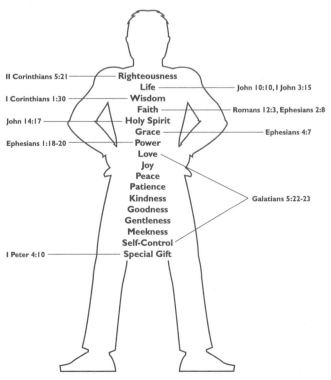

II Corinthians 5:21 — Righteousness
Life — John 10:10, I John 3:15
I Corinthians 1:30 — Wisdom
Faith — Romans 12:3, Ephesians 2:8
John 14:17 — Holy Spirit
Grace — Ephesians 4:7
Ephesians 1:18-20 — Power
Love
Joy
Peace
Patience
Kindness — Galatians 5:22-23
Goodness
Gentleness
Meekness
Self-Control
I Peter 4:10 — Special Gift

Leadership starts
from within.
It's *being*
before *doing*.

Studying this little diagram transformed my sense of identity. I began to believe what was already true about me, but it changed the way I led others. If it helps, use it.

Question: *What can you do to ensure your self-image reflects your identity in Christ as you minister on the campus, in your church, with your family?*

Why would anyone else want to follow us until we have overcome our own flesh, our laziness, our whims, and our knee-jerk reactions

Personal Discipline

A second issue we must settle in self-leadership is personal discipline. Why would anyone else want to follow us until we have overcome our own flesh, our laziness, our whims, and our knee-jerk reactions. If you don't have your own house in order, how do you expect others to let you manage theirs? This is the priority the apostle Paul highlighted in 1 Timothy 3:5. A leader with self-discipline lives out the convictions he or she espouses and gains credibility among the people who watch. As a campus leader your integrity produces trust.

This is the campus leader's journey of discipline. The divine process is in three stages:

> The emerging leader submits to discipline from without.
> Then he or she establishes discipline within.
> Finally he or she is permitted to establish discipline for others.

A campus leader is a person who has learned to obey a discipline imposed from without, and has then taken on a more rigorous discipline from within. Those who rebel against authority, scorn self-discipline; shirk the rigors and turn from the sacrifices do not qualify to lead. This was Paul's testimony in 1 Corinthians 9:24-27 (HCSB®):

"Do you not know that the runners in a stadium all race, but only one receives the prize? Run in such a way that you may win. Now everyone who competes exercises self-control in everything. However, they do it to receive a perishable crown, but we an imperishable one. Therefore, I do not run like one who runs aimlessly, or box like one who beats the air. Instead, I discipline my body and bring it under strict control, so that after preaching to others, I myself will not be disqualified."

Richard Foster, in his book *The Celebration of Discipline,* places the spiritual disciplines into three categories to help us better understand them:

The Inward Disciplines
Meditation	Fasting
Prayer	Bible Study

The Outward Disciplines
Simplicity	Submission
Solitude	Service

The Corporate Disciplines
Confession	Guidance
Worship	Celebration

For many, the big temptation is to take shortcuts on discipline. You may remember the story of the millionaire who gave a large sum of money to a building contractor, and asked him to build a house. He said, "Here is plenty of cash for the project. You won't need all of it, but I don't want you to run out. When you are finished, whatever money you have left over, you can keep it."

The contractor's eyes got big, because he knew he could build this house for next to nothing and have loads of cash left over. So he began building. He took all kinds of shortcuts—putting studs four feet apart; using only one nail per board; and putting only one coat of paint on the walls. Needless to say, he finished quickly and returned to the millionaire with the keys to the house. He had a big wad of money left in his pocket. But when the contractor handed over the keys—the millionaire said, "Oh, I forgot to tell you. The house is yours!"

What a picture this can be of our lives today. We take shortcuts thinking we can get ahead, and God whispers from heaven: "It's your life you are building."

These disciplines are what carry you as a campus leader over the long haul. Your charisma may attract student, faculty, administrators, and pastors to your ministry, but your character will keep them. These disciplines are not designed to quench your lifestyle and your spirit. Just the opposite: they will enable you to experience a growing relationship with Jesus more so than you would without them. I'll put it this way: our conversion and our walk with God are like a wedding and a marriage.

Conversion = the grace of a beautiful wedding.

Spiritual disciplines = the labor of a healthy, intimate marriage.

Like so many failing marriages, probably 90% of all Christians need to rescue their spiritual lives from the tyranny of feelings. Once we incorporate discipline into our lives, we are free to obey God because we have what it takes to do so. It is different than legalism. Legalism is changing from the outside in. Discipline is changing from the inside out. It isn't about adding new things to do to an already busy life. It is incorporating a priority into a lifestyle, so that it becomes a natural part of who we are.

For example, it is difficult for tennis player Pete Sampras to make a bad shot on the court. He would have to work hard to play poorly. Why? Because for years he has gone out and stroked that tennis ball over and over until it is a part of his game. Now he doesn't even have to try to play well. It comes naturally. So it is with a campus leader's discipline.

Question: *What disciplines do you need to incorporate into your life? When will you do so?*

Emotional Security

When campus leaders (full-time, part-time, volunteer teacher) have emotional deficits, they eventually sabotage their own leadership. Others around you will withdraw. They sense the leader is unstable. And they are right. Insecurity is the cause of more leadership breakdowns than anything else. Emotional stability is the infrastructure that holds up a leader in crisis.

In 1995, Daniel Goleman wrote a best-selling book called *Emotional Intelligence*. Since that book was released, Goleman has spent his time analyzing why some leaders develop to their fullest potential and why most hit a plateau far from their full potential. His conclusion? The difference is (you guessed it) self-leadership. He calls it "emotional self control." What characterizes maximum leadership potential according to Goleman? Tenaciously staying in leadership despite overwhelming opposition or discouragement. Remaining sober-minded during crisis. Staying focused on the mission instead of being distracted by someone else's agenda. All these indicate high levels of emotional self-control. Goleman says, "Exceptional leaders distinguish themselves because of superior self-leadership."[3]

Just two weeks after I became a youth pastor, the senior pastor called me into his office because he "had to share some things with me." I was all ears. I was not prepared for what he

Our big temptation is to take shortcuts on discipline.

Discipline is changing from the inside out.

Emotional stability is the infrastructure that holds up a leader in crisis.

told me. He said, "Tim, I feel I should tell you that the people in this church intimidate me."

I gave him a puzzled look. "You mean the congregation you speak to every week threatens you?" I asked. That's exactly what he was saying. Then he continued: "You should also know that the board at this church intimidates me."

"Really?" I said. "The guys you make decisions with every month around a table, the ones you laugh with and go to dinner with—they intimidate you?"

"I know it sounds strange." He paused. "But there's one more thing." He paused again: "Tim, you intimidate me."

I sat there stunned. I was a college-aged punk pastor working with students. How in the world could I intimidate this guy in mid-life? For that matter, how could these people he loved and shepherded shake him up so badly? I had to ask. His answer was eye-opening. He explained that he never really had good self-esteem. He had toyed with other career paths, but decided on ministry because he enjoyed the audience it would give him. He tended to over-compensate for his uncertainty by being loud and humorous. But it was a cover-up. He was an insecure person, and those deficits were now showing. I believe everyone has pockets of insecurity, but leadership roles work like a magnifying glass on them. Our deficits go on display in front of many.

I believe everyone has
pockets of insecurity,
but leadership roles
work like a magnifying
glass on them.

Self-leadership is work, and nobody can do that work for you. You have to do this work yourself. It is so tough that most leaders avoid it. Instead, we try to inspire or control our people than to do the rigorous work of self-reflection. Eventually, we ruin things. Back in 1987-88, when so many Christian leaders were falling morally, a survey was taken. Several hundred pastors were interviewed who had compromised their integrity, fallen into sin, and lost their ministry. Three consistent observations were made when they responded to the question: "How could you do it?" The top three responses were:

- I had stopped spending time alone with God each day.
- I had no accountability to others in my life.
- I never thought this kind of sin and failure could happen to me.

They were blindsided. One top Christian leader who disqualified himself from ministry was the subject of a magazine article. The story read, "He sank like a rock, beat up, burned out, angry and depressed, no good to himself, and no good to the people he loved." This can happen to any campus worker.

The best gift
you can give
the people you lead
is a healthy,
energized,
fully surrendered,
focused self.

When this pastor finally wrote publicly about this experience, he said, "Eventually I couldn't even sleep at night. Another wave of broken lives would come to shore at the church, and I found I didn't have enough compassion for them anymore. And inside I became angry, angry, angry. Many people still wonder whatever happened to me. They think I had a crisis of faith. The fact is, I simply collapsed on the inside."[4]

It's been said before and I will say it here. The best gift you can give the students and others you lead is a healthy, energized, fully surrendered, focused self. When we fail the self-leadership test, we will often begin getting defensive or start playing games. These games sap our energy until we finally collapse.

The most common symptoms of insecurity are:
1. Comparison—You compare yourself to others and score yourself against their achievements.
2. Compensation—You feel like a victim and now must compensate for your losses or inferiority.

3. Competition—You drift into self-centered patterns, consumed by outdoing others, in receiving attention or reward.

4. Compulsion—You are driven to perform to gain others' approval; you are a people pleaser.

5. Condemnation—You become judgmental with yourself or others, resulting in either self-pity or self-conceit.

6. Control—In order to validate your worth, you feel you must take charge to protect yourself, promote yourself, and monopolize situations.

Three Steps into the Truth

Obviously, these games are based on lies. The truth makes us free, but lies put us in bondage. The lies are especially degrading in the ministry. If we're going to have the energy on campus to give to Christ's kingdom, we must become emotionally secure leaders.

Try this three-step process when you struggle with insecurity as a campus worker:

- Determine the trigger event that fostered the lie or bondage.
- Discover the lie you've believed about that situation.
- Decide what response is truthful, appropriate, and realistic.

Question: *When do your insecurities show up most? What lie have you believed when you feel insecure? What's the truth that you must remind yourself?*

Core Values

A final issue we must settle is the area of our core values. Self-leadership must always be based on a set of values you hold to the core of your heart. Campus leaders must be principle centered. You can't drift with the culture and change the foundation on which you stand morally or spiritually. Our core values are the horsepower that drive each decision we make. They define who we are as campus leaders. They are like the rudder on a ship that keeps it on course, even in storms. Values include ethics and truths we stand on and stand for.

For each of us, they must be biblical. They should reflect God's heart for the Great Commission and the great commandment. Experts on this subject suggest that we can't have large quantities of "core values." In fact, if we have more than six, they aren't core. Years ago I came up with a set of six values that guide my life. They are amazing accountability partners for me as I say Yes and No to opportunities that arise. My wife and I came up with a set of family core values five years ago. They guide the way we govern our home. My hope is that even if we never spoke about them, our children could identify them when they leave our home at 18 because we lived them before their eyes.

Let me suggest a profound truth. Both vision and values are important to effective campus leaders. However, values have priority over vision. Here's why. You can tell students your goals for ministry growth, but without an environment where corresponding values are displayed, the results will be short-lived. They're synthetic. Incarnated values lead to accomplished vision. Truett Cathy, founder of Chick-Fil-A restaurants, says it this way: "My attitude regarding the distant future is to do the best we can every day and take advantage of unexpected opportunities. That combination will lead us to success. I don't want to set some arbitrary target out there that might lead us to make inappropriate decisions just to achieve it."[5]

Hmmm.

Sounds like the Scriptures. Jesus told us we must get the tree right, then the fruit will be right (Matt. 12:33-35). I believe if we incarnate the values well, the vision will be reached. Case in

The truth makes us free, but lies put us in bondage.

Our core values are the horsepower that drive each decision we make.

Incarnated values lead to accomplished vision.

point: the Book of Acts. There was never an evangelism seminar in the Book. We see no evidence that the disciples set some numerical goal for church growth. Instead, they focused on quality of ministry to the world. They met needs and helped people connect with Jesus. Church growth was not a goal but a by-product. Healthy things naturally grow.

God's vision is to reach the world, including college campuses around the world. Christ said so in Matthew 28:18-20. His method for accomplishing this vision, however, is valuing the individual. Christ said so in Luke 15:3-10. He spoke of the lost coin, the lost sheep, and ultimately the lost son. If we value the one, the world will be won. We need the vision to point us in the right direction, and we need the values to help us get there in a Christ-honoring way.

The Great Wall of China is one of the Seven Wonders of the World. Its early history is interesting. It was originally built centuries ago to keep out all invading armies. It was built so tall and so wide, no enemy could penetrate it. At least, that's what they thought. The Chinese were successfully invaded three times in the first 100 years. In none of those instances, however, did the enemy climb the wall, dig under it, or tunnel through it. In every case, they simply bribed the guards at the gate.

What a picture of having a vision with no values. The vision for protecting China by building a great wall was great. Unfortunately, the young men guarding the gates of that wall had weak character. Chinese leaders should have spent as much time building their character as they did the wall.

Question: *How do you define success in your life? What are your core values?*

Assessment

The final section of this chapter will give you a chance to evaluate yourself. Review the diagram below, called "My Network" and fill in the names of people who fit each role. These represent healthy relationships all campus leaders need. Examine where you have voids.

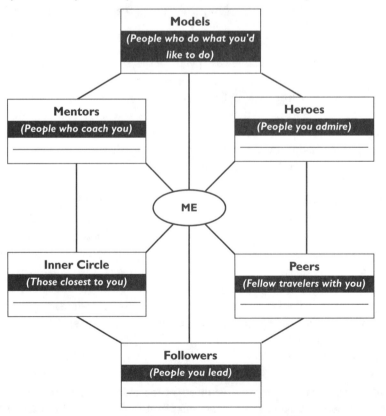

Church growth was not a goal but a by-product.

Alarm Bells for Campus Ministers

Doran McCarty has created a grid evaluation for ministers I will recommend at the end of this chapter. He and others inspired me to create some criteria for healthy leadership. The following questions are good to ask yourself and others for accountability. These are critical issues for one who is a spiritual leader on the campus. Unhealthy responses should signal an alarm and a call to action.

1. Competence—What is my capacity for work? Where is my strength? Do I get the job done?

2. Passion—Is my passion hot? Do I energize others by my leadership? What's my energy level?

3. Authority—Am I submitted to someone in authority? Who is it? How do I handle accountability?

4. Spiritual Life—Is my personal walk with God up-to-date? Do I model intimacy and obedience to God?

5. Motives—Why do I do what I do? How do I pursue my goals? Do I seek personal gain?

6. Perspective—Do I listen to what God is saying to the whole body of Christ? Do I have a kingdom mindset?

7. Initiative—Do I start projects or tend to wait on others to take charge? Do I pioneer with no structure?

8. Discipline—Do I keep my priorities straight? Do I live out what I say is important? Am I in charge of my time, energy, and resources?

9. Identity—How do I perceive myself in relation to others? Am I secure in who I am? Am I aware of my weaknesses?

10. Conflict—Do I experience conflict with others regularly? How do I handle differences?

11. Agenda—Do I have personal, hidden agendas? Am I a loner in ministry? Am I concerned with building my image?

12. Emotional security—Am I overly impressed by flattery or criticism? Do I get defensive? Am I swayed too much by human opinion?

13. Risk—Can I move into areas where the outcome is uncertain? Do I resist change or vulnerability?

14. Values—Do I live by personal core values? Have I established values for my ministry on campus/church?

15. Calling—Is my calling for campus work sure? Does my call to reach students give me focus and passion to serve God?

The inward life of a campus leader in any capacity is not only central, it must be the priority. We must travel within before we can travel without. Stephen Covey communicates the importance of this character journey in the following passage:

> The inward life of a campus leader in any capacity is not only central, it must be the priority.

"If I try to use human influence strategies and tactics of how to get other people to do what I want, to work better, to be more motivated, to like me and each other—while my character is fundamentally flawed, marked by duplicity or insincerity—then, in the long run, I cannot be successful. My duplicity will breed distrust, and everything I do, even using so-called good human relations techniques will be perceived as manipulative.

"It simply makes no difference how good the rhetoric is or even how good the intentions are; if there is little trust, there is no foundation for permanent success. Only basic goodness gives life to technique."[7]

Further Reading

Like a Rock, Andy Stanley, Thomas Nelson Publishers, 1997

Emotional Intelligence, Daniel Goleman, Bantam Books, 1997

Overcoming the Dark Side of Leadership, Gary McIntosh & Samuel Rima, Baker Book House, 1997

Leadership and Self Deception, The Arbinger Institute, Berrett-Koehler Publishers, 2002

The Other Side of Leadership, Eugene Habecker, Chariot Victor Books, 1987

Portrait of a Leader, book one, The Spiritual Formation of a Leader, Tim Elmore, EQUIP/Growing Leaders, 2000

I Like Your Style

ASSESSING YOUR LEADERSHIP IDENTITY

*"Your speech should always be gracious, seasoned with salt,
so that you may know how you should answer each person."*
—Colossians 4:6 (HCSB®)

"Success is a process of becoming who you already are."—Frank Potts

Gary is a friend of mine who, upon his graduation, went into campus ministry. He loves college students and knew how to connect with them immediately. He worked for eight years and had great success at a major university in the south. His ministry grew, his budget went up, and excitement among the students was high. After eight years, however, he decided it was time for him to move on. He felt he'd done what God had called him to do there, and he was ready for a new challenge. He moved to a school in the midwest, and took charge of a ministry there. He decided to try the same strategy he'd used before. He implemented his wildly successful Bible studies, discipleship groups, and ministry programs quickly.

To say the programs failed would be an understatement. Gary was a flop. I spoke to him over the phone and he was close to tears about it. How could he be so successful on one campus with these programs and plans, then fail so miserably on another? Within a year, folks drew the conclusion that he was a mediocre leader, and he questioned his own call into the ministry. He decided to quit.

It took Gary months to recover from this experience. What a sad commentary on a misplaced leader, strategy, people, and time. If only Gary had understood his leadership identity. If only he'd recognized which parts of his leadership style were adaptable and which were not. Then he could have made a wiser decision on where he would best fit.

> There are, in fact, many leadership styles that work, both in the marketplace and in the ministry.

There's More Than One Way to Do It

It used to be that leadership and management researchers all seemed to believe that if you were going to grow an organization, you had to possess a certain temperament, perform a set number of essential functions, and even embrace a particular style of leadership. In short, all good leaders look basically alike.

Very few experts believe that anymore. Peter Drucker recently said he doesn't believe there is "one right style" of leadership that will do the trick. There are, in fact, many leadership styles that work, both in the marketplace and in the ministry. Dr. John Maxwell once remarked, "We must size up every situation we face, then decide on what leadership approach is best. In other words, read the situation before you lead the situation." I concur. It is ridiculous to think we must "clone" ourselves to look like someone else, because they happened to succeed in their context. Here is the key:

> It is essential that we discover our natural leadership identity, then determine how we can strengthen and balance that identity as our context demands it.

When you consider your own personality and leadership style, in which situations do you believe you best fit? Jot several ideas in the space provided below.

What are the leadership contexts in which you tend to flourish, especially as you work with college students? Jot several thoughts in the space below.

I believe leadership success is about 50% nature and 50% nurture. By this I mean, it's half about the wiring God gave you and finding a match for who you are; and it's half about adapting yourself to your environment so that you can be fruitful.

Because leading students today is so complex and because the campus is constantly changing, I believe it's crucial to be principle-centered, driven by core values that will not change. Campus leaders need a strong philosophical/spiritual base. You need to know who you are and what you stand for.

In addition, however, you need to be ready to adapt almost everything else. Your approach to relationships, your mode of directing a group of people, your methods, and your style of leadership may all need to change in order to connect in a new environment. Being effective is half about knowing your identity (which cannot change), and half about knowing all the other facets of your leadership, which can change.

If Gary had been able to do this, his ministry experience might have been vastly different. First of all, it may have helped him to realize he didn't fit as well leading a campus ministry in the midwest. Or it may have helped him to see that his core values fit, but that he would need to adapt in many other ways to make his new position work. Doing the same old thing can ruin our leadership. We may have to take risks—which means we'd better know what we're willing to risk and what we aren't. In an old episode of the television show "MASH," Hawkeye Pierce, a doctor played by Alan Alda, reflected: "Sometimes you have to leave the city of your comfort and go into the wilderness of your intuition. You can't get to there by bus, only by hard work and risk, and by not quite knowing what you're doing. But what you'll discover will be wonderful. What you'll discover will be yourself."

> Being effective is half about knowing your identity(which cannot change), and half about knowing all the other facets of your leadership, which can change.

The Evolution of Leadership

In order to discover your leadership identity, we'll first discuss leadership, then we'll assess identity. Leadership is a buzzword today. Many people are writing on the subject. However, as you know, there is not much written specially for collegiate leadership for leaders. It is important to note that the subject of leadership has experienced an evolution over the years. While we have always needed spiritual leaders, the style of leader we want is different now.

In fact, over the last 50 years our world transitioned in the way it views leadership. The acceptable style has changed for most people. The way we led in 1950 looks a little different than the way we might lead today on the campus. Our culture has demanded it. Let's take a look at this evolution.

Up to 1950s	1960s-1970s	1980s	1990s	Today
Military Commander	CEO	Entrepreneur	Coach	Poet/ Gardener

Military Commander

Up until the 1950s, the acceptable style—the popular style for most leaders—was the military commander style. Regardless of whether it was a business, church, campus, or government position, leaders led in a very top-down fashion. Flow charts told everyone where they fit, and if you weren't at the top of the chart, you didn't lead. Leaders led and followers followed. Folks didn't question authority like we do today. Leaders controlled the information. It was a black-and-white issue. Even our presidents during this period came from military backgrounds where this style was common: Dwight Eisenhower and John F. Kennedy. There was one leader in the organization.

The key value during this period was loyalty. Employers expected employees to be loyal and stay in the factory 40 years, get a gold watch, then retire. If someone left a staff position, they were considered disloyal. Parishioners didn't leave churches because they were loyal to a denomination. Pastors enjoyed the respect of most people, even outside of the church; they were considered an authority. One reason for the acceptance of this style was the level of education of most people. Relatively few went to college. During the 20s and 30s, an eighth-grade education was considered an achievement. By the 50s, a high-school degree was the norm. Only leaders had access to information. This is no longer true in our "information age." Consequently, during this time, most leaders enjoyed leading from their positional authority.

Chief Executive Officer

By the late 60s, America was changing. Riots on university campuses, civil-rights marches on the streets, and baby-boomer rebels began to question the idea of blind submission to leaders. "Question Authority" was a common bumper sticker. To make things worse, by the late 60s, it became clear that President Johnson had not been honest with Americans about the Vietnam war. He kept saying all was well, but it wasn't. Add to that the Watergate scandal of President Nixon, and you understand why the common leadership style could no longer be "military commander." Few were interested in blind submission. Followers were asking questions and leaders had to begin explaining what they were doing and why. The new image for leadership was the CEO (Chief Executive Officer). They led by casting vision to their people, in hope that their followers would buy in to the vision and work toward its fulfillment. The CEO style became popular not only in business, where you would expect it, but also in non-profits and government circles too.

The key value during this period was productivity. If the organization's goal was to make widgets in a factory, the CEO-style leader would motivate his people to make more and better widgets. Advertising and marketing began to play a major role as large numbers of corporations went nationwide. Productivity was the watchword. Business leaders even became popular during this time. Why? They led from vision, not just from positional authority. While this was an improvement, it was still very top-down in nature.

Entrepreneur

By the 80s, a new style of leader became popular. It fit the era in which we lived as Americans felt our nation was becoming great again—in industry versus the Japanese, in the military versus the USSR, and even in the religious world as mega-churches became more numerous and popular during this period. The style we celebrated was the leader as an entrepreneur. He or she was a pioneer; had few boundaries; didn't do things the conventional way; and managed "by walking around," as Tom Peters reported. This leader, in fact, actually looked for non-traditional ways to lead. It was the Reagan era...the Lee Iacocca era...the Chuck Swindoll era.

> Folks didn't question authority like we do today.

The key value during this period was innovation. Good leaders felt the most critical element of their leadership was being the first to do it. Think about it: fax machines, computers, walk-mans, and videos all became popular during this decade. Certainly, innovation is still a revered quality among leaders today, but it was during this period we came to grips with how important it was. Because society began changing at such a fast rate, leaders had to be out in front, and questioning the way they did things every year. They led from creativity during this season. The effective leader made sure nothing was sacred if it didn't work. The emerging work force was looking for this new kind of leader—someone who would lead from creativity. This innovative style enabled followers to share ideas that might be implemented by the organization. This helped them tolerate the fact that this leadership style was still a top-down model.

Coach

By 1990, a new style became popular. It was the leader as a coach, and it remains a common style today. This style was appealing to Generation X, who was now entering the work force in large numbers—and who longed for relationships and authenticity. They didn't care for an effective, productive leader who was untouchable. Unlike their baby-boomer parents who lived to work, they simply worked to live. The new kind of leader had to know how to assemble and work with teams of people. By this time, business leaders even began creating work environments to be conducive for teamwork and relationships. Many put coffeehouses in their office, sofas, VCRs, and sometimes even video games for employee break times.

The leader as a coach valued teamwork and morale. They saw themselves as coaches who had players. Those players each had strengths, and it was the job of the leader to be a broker of those strengths and talents. The leader had to find the proper roles for all the players, so they could make their significant contribution to the team. Although this style was more participatory, it was still top-down in nature. Leaders led through placement of their people in roles that would both fulfill the organization's goals and fulfill the player.

Poet/Gardener

As we proceed into the 21st century, I see a new kind of leader on the horizon. He/she is a leader who's in touch with the postmodern world in which we live. This leader combines many of the strengths of the last four styles. In addition, he or she is secure enough to build relationships with their team, and drive the process toward getting the desired result. We'll call this type of leader a poet and a gardener.

This new generation of leaders doesn't enter their position assuming they have all the answers. In fact, they surround themselves with a team of other leaders (not just a team of players, but a leadership team). This inner circle is optimally diverse in their strengths and perspectives, but not in their values. As this team meets to discuss ideas, the poet/gardener listens and adds, then ultimately puts words to what the Holy Spirit seems to be saying to the group. I call these leaders poets because they are discerning of the culture and the ideas that emerge from others, not just their own. In the same way we enjoy a poem because that poet put words to what we were feeling and thinking, this leader summarizes big-picture ideas with excellence. They synthesize and extrapolate thoughts, then come up with the best one, even if it is not their own. At this point, they become a wordsmith who articulates the idea until the entire team owns it. They give language to the ideas and feelings the people possess. While the leader-poet has many good ideas, they don't pretend to think up all the answers, and the pressure is off them to do so. They are communicators of the best ideas, regardless of the source. They recognize that people no longer rely on a leader to gain information—it's accessible to all. Needless to say, these leaders are attractive to a new workforce who longs to be part of creating the ideas and determining the direction. People support what they help create.

The leader-gardeners are people-developers. The work of a gardener is to cultivate the soil, pull the weeds, and create an environment in which plants can grow. In fact, this is the primary function of a gardener. In this same way, the leader-gardener sees the primary function of their

Good leaders led from vision, not just from positional authority.

The leader as a coach valued teamwork and morale.

This new generation of leaders are communicators of the best ideas, regardless of the source.

leadership to be developing their people, not simply doing the program. They are equippers. They empower. These kind of leaders see themselves as mentors to their team. Relationship is inherent in this style of leadership. It causes employees to want to stick around because they see the value in staying. They will not only help the organization get to the goal, they will grow in the process. The employee doesn't merely feel like a number or a cog in the wheel. They are "used" by their boss—they are developed, and God uses them in the process.

The key values for the poet/gardener are connection and growth. These leaders connect with their people and their culture. This connection actually creates the culture within their organization. They are in touch. They also value growth—not just organizationally but for each individual in it. They resource everyone. Personal growth is what the leader values for each team member. They lead out of shared ownership. Everyone owns the vision and they flourish as they move toward it.

I believe this is the attractive leader of today. This isn't to say all the others will die out. Based on temperament and generation, other styles will remain, and some will do well because of the strength of the leader's personality and vision. But the style that the new generation of employees will want is the poet/gardener. No doubt, certain crisis situations may demand a different style. On September 11, 2001, we didn't need President Bush to form a focus group to discuss our feelings about terrorists. We needed a military commander-style in that moment. There will be situations where each of these styles will be appropriate on your campus and church. However, over the years, there's been an evolution. People have desired less formality and more relationship. As a rule, most healthy students are hungry for the poet/gardener leadership style.

As our perspective on leadership has evolved from military commander to poet/gardener, the style of leader we value has changed. The qualities we value have remained constant (integrity, purpose, wisdom, and so forth) but the style is different. The healthy poet/gardener possesses these qualities:

- More highly relational
- Interprets culture and reflects well
- Emotionally secure
- Shares ownership freely
- Empowers others well

- Comfortable with uncertainty
- Listens and fosters self-discovery
- Embraces the role of a mentor
- Less formal in structure
- Driven by service more than ego

Question: *Which style have you seen as a follower? Which do you practice as a leader with your students? with the faculty/administrators? with other campus leaders/church leaders in your community?*

Who Do You Think You Are?

A few years ago something humorous arose out of a desperate situation. A crowded flight was cancelled at Denver's International Airport. The passengers formed a line at another gate trying to get on the next available flight. The line was extremely long. One man who didn't want to wait crowded to the front and demanded the clerk issue him a ticket. She smiled and said she would do what she could, but that he would have to wait in line with everyone else. The impatient man didn't like this response and insisted she should make an exception in his case. When she told him again he would have to go to the end of the line, he lost his composure. He leaned across the counter and asked, "Ma'am. Do you know who I am?" With poise, the clerk walked back to the intercom and requested help from her staff. She said: "May I get some help at Gate B22. There is a man here who doesn't know who he is!"

Truth is funnier than fiction. I have a similar question for you as a campus leader in what role you play. Do you know who you are? As the story above humorously illustrates, we need to

They lead out of shared ownership.

As a rule, most healthy employees are hungry for the poet/gardener leadership style.

know who we are before we can get anywhere in our leadership on campus. It really helps to nail this down before we can lead others effectively. I believe there are a variety of factors that influence our leadership identity and style. As I have already mentioned, these factors are derived from both nature and nurture. Below I've listed six primary factors that will determine who you are and how you act as a campus leader. Evaluate yourself as you read them.

Let's evaluate:

Your Perspective

You bring a certain perspective to your campus leadership role that impacts the way you lead. This will include your cumulative attitudes about leadership. These attitudes are drawn from your past models, your sense of personal security and identity, your people skills, and your notions about leading. Your perspective on leadership may be affected by your early environment., perhaps formed as a student observing a spiritual leader on campus. This perspective becomes the inward bent and angle you have on how you will influence your followers to accomplish a task. The primary difference between followers and leaders is perspective.

What perspective on campus leadership do you possess?

Your Personality

One of the greatest factors determining your leadership identity on campus or in the church is your natural temperament or personality. This is your genetic make-up, drawn from your family tree. Are you a people person or an analyst? Are you loud or soft spoken? Are you a driver, a diplomat, or a dreamer? Your personality affects how you naturally approach both projects and students and others on campus. It includes your temperament, character, tastes and preferences, and God-given abilities. To summarize, it's your internal resources.

What's your personality style and how does it affect the way you lead in your campus program?

Your Position

While leadership doesn't require you to have a position, your leadership position will be another factor you'll need to examine. By this, I mean: what is the context in which you lead? What levels of authority do you possess? What is the task you must accomplish? What are the structures of support? What are the resources you have to work with? What systems are in place that cannot be changed? All of your answers must be factored into the equation, in order to determine how you will lead.

How does your position as a campus minister affect the way you lead? How you submit to authority on the campus and in the church?

Your People

Still another factor that influences your leadership identity is the people who you will lead. Do you have mature or immature followers? Are they prepared for the task that must be achieved? Do they possess the gifts necessary? Do they own the vision for your campus program? Are they similar to you, as a leader, or very dissimilar to you? Clearly, the followers you have to work with must, at least partially, determine how you will lead, and how fast you can move as you attempt to take them to the destination. Sometimes the people have unspoken but very real expectations that will impact the way you lead.

Who are your people? How have they impacted the way you lead?

Your Purpose

Another obvious factor on how you approach your leadership role on campus and with students will be the purpose you've embraced for your organization and for yourself. Often our leadership approaches change when our objectives change. When a leader finds an organization whose mission and purpose strongly overlap with theirs, there will be natural momentum. The activity will become more intense, energized, and fluid. This momentum can be predicted when the leader's personal passion coincides with the needs of the organization.

What's your purpose and how does it affect your drive and methods as a campus leader?

Your Pressure

A final primary factor that I believe determines your leadership identity in any given situation is the amount of pressure involved in the task. I have watched good leaders crumble as they took on new responsibility that they had never faced before, and the pressure alone seemed to make them different leaders. It determined their confidence, security, defensive attitudes, risk taking, and so forth. They were like Dr. Jekyll and Mr. Hyde. The pressure literally changed their leadership identity and approach.

How do you handle pressure? What does pressure do to your campus leadership?

If your responses to the simple list above are discouraging, take heart. Whether you feel like a natural leader or not, you can change. All of the above factors, except one—your personality—can change and improve. Let's move on now to another evaluation.

Your Attraction Assets

For decades now, our world has measured the "intelligence quotient" (I.Q.) of people. While this is certainly important, I believe there is a more important measuring stick when it comes to leadership: our Influence Quotient. Our Influence Quotient is determined by our attraction assets that we possess and offer to students and others on campus and in the church.

- Passion & Enthusiasm—Possessing an energy and excitement that propels you and encourages those around you to action

- Insight & Wisdom—Having discernment and an intuitive understanding into students and situations

- Relational Charisma—Possessing a warm and magnetic personality

- Productive Ability—Accomplishing tasks efficiently and thoroughly; being capable of getting the job done with your students

- Character & Courage—Doing what is right in your role on campus even when it is difficult

- Communication Skills—Expressing your thoughts and ideas clearly, which motivates students to act

- Gifts & Talents—Possessing natural abilities, spiritual gifts, and cultivated skills that compel others to join

People follow leaders based upon their IQ (Influence Quotient), and IQ depends upon how many (amount) and how much (volume) of the following "attraction assets" exist inside of them. Rate yourself based on the list following (1 being lowest, 10 being highest).

> The pressure literally changed their leadership identity and approach.

ATTRACTION ASSET	VOLUME									
Passion & Enthusiasm	1	2	3	4	5	6	7	8	9	10
Insight & Wisdom	1	2	3	4	5	6	7	8	9	10
Relational Charisma	1	2	3	4	5	6	7	8	9	10
Productive Ability	1	2	3	4	5	6	7	8	9	10
Character & Courage	1	2	3	4	5	6	7	8	9	10
Communication Skills	1	2	3	4	5	6	7	8	9	10
Gifts & Talents	1	2	3	4	5	6	7	8	9	10

> The $50,000 question is: What's the primary reason people follow you?

Which are your strongest assets for your ministry? Which are your weakest? Are there any you do not possess? How do you think this will affect your ability to attract followers in your ministry? What do you think you will have to do to make up for what you lack in certain areas to have a successful ministry on campus?

No doubt, the more the attraction assets you possess, the more likely you will attract student followers, and the more likely you will attract a variety of followers. Students on campus follow leaders for a reason, and as leaders, we want to give them as many reasons to follow as we can. Usually, there are one or two primary reasons why a follower is attracted to a leader. Note the list of biblical leaders below, and speculate with me whether followers might have followed them due to the assets I have indicated:

Biblical Leaders

Assets	Leaders Who Possessed This
1. Passion & Enthusiasm	David, Elijah, Peter
2. Insight & Wisdom	Solomon, Samuel, Ezra
3. Relational Charisma	Barnabas, Apollos, John
4. Productive Ability	Nehemiah, Paul, Titus
5. Character & Courage	Moses, Daniel, Joshua
6. Communication Skills	Jeremiah, Amos, Isaiah
7. Gifts & Talents	Samson, Elisha, Joseph

Question: *We have examined some factors that influence your leadership identity. The $50,000 question is: What's the primary reason students follow you? Take a few moments and reflect on your answer.*

Why Michelangelo was so picky, picky, picky...
Italian artist Michelangelo was said to have taken a huge amount of time selecting the marble to use to carve his statue of David. Someone asked why he took so long. He responded that the raw material he chose would determine much about how the finished product would look. So it is with us. The raw material God has given us will have a large affect on the kind of leadership approach we adopt in our campus leadership. By recognizing our raw material, we will better understand where we are most suited to lead, and where we must adapt to reach the goals we want to reach. We begin to be comfortable with the person God made us to be.

> "Every man starts with all there is."
> —Henry Ford

Once a distinguished visitor to Henry Ford's auto plant met him after an exhaustive tour of the factory. The visitor was lost in wonder and admiration. "It seems almost impossible, Mr. Ford," he told the industrialist, "that a man, starting 25 years ago with practically nothing, could accomplish all this."

"You say that I started with practically nothing," Ford replied, "but that's hardly correct. Every man starts with all there is." Then Ford pointed to his heart. "Everything is here—the essence and substance of all there is."

Your Natural Approach

Now that we've examined the primary factors that influence our leadership identity, let's take a look at how this is applied to our ministries on campus and in the church. Given these factors, how do we tend to naturally cast a vision, solve a problem, motivate workers, or attack a leadership task?

Knowing your natural tendencies will help both you and your team. We all have strengths and weaknesses that need to be complimented. I was part of a group that was brainstorming solutions to a problem we faced. Although I was in charge, everyone had a different opinion on how we could solve our dilemma. One person suggested we organize our committee differently. Another said we needed to focus more on building relationships and shepherding each other. A third made me feel totally guilty by saying we needed to pray more. That would solve our problems. Ouch! Can you identify with this situation? Which leader was right?

It wasn't until later that it became clear—none of the ideas were wrong. However, it was helpful to recognize that we were all simply perceiving the circumstances through the eyes of our spiritual gifts and personality. This is the beauty of the body of Christ. Everyone was prepared to make their contribution based on what they had to offer. Someone once said, "When all you have is a hammer, the whole world looks like a nail."

My premise or assumption is that every campus leader brings with them approaches to ministry from both genetics and environment. In the following list, we'll examine your natural "style" and what that means to both your strengths and weaknesses. Generally speaking, a leader is strong in one of two extremes, in each category on this list. It is optimal to work toward a mature balance in each. However, we usually don't begin our journey with that balance, nor do we achieve it without deliberate action steps. Often, balance will require a mentor in our lives to enable us to see things objectively. Where we are weak, we will want to work to adjust and equalize our skills. Remember: the key is to walk the center of tension between the two extremes. Evaluate yourself, based on the list below. Score yourself by putting a mark on each scale. Then discuss it with someone who understands campus ministry.

> We were all simply perceiving the circumstances through the eyes of our spiritual gifts and personality.

1. **Category: Management. The leader is either...**
   Relationship Oriented or Result Oriented
   This means that as a leader on campus you will have a tendency to build relationship in order to succeed, or to focus on achieving results. As a leader you will either be people-driven or product–driven.

   Relationship I————————————————————————————————I Result

2. **Category: Communication. The leader is either...**
   Passion Based or Substance Based
   When communicating ideas as a collegiate leader, you will rely on your passion to deliver the idea, or on the content of the idea itself. Your style will depend on your ability to express yourself or on the research/information.

   Passion I————————————————————————————————I Substance

3. Category: Vision. The leader is either an...
Adopter of Dreams or Adapter of Dreams

Your leadership style will either rely completely on obtaining someone else's ideas, or you'll insist on using only "your own ideas." You either steal or must adapt ideas to make them your own.

Adopter |————————————————————————————| Adapter

4. Category: Delegation. The leader is either...
Detail Reliant or Charisma Reliant

As a collegiate leader, you will either depend on your ability to organize details, and thus win trust, or rely on your ability to provide high morale and motivation to your students and other workers.

Detail |————————————————————————————| Charisma

5. Category: Priorities and Decision Making. The leader is either...
Publicly Visible or Publicly Beneficial

This is more difficult to sort out. This style of collegiate leader will either prioritize your agenda around what students "see" (immediate felt needs) or what's most advantageous for them (real needs).

Visible |————————————————————————————| Beneficial

6. Category: Empowering Staff. The leader is either...
Visual or Verbal

When it comes to empowering staff, if you are this type of leader on your campus you will either lean on your ability to model what you want, or to speak words of affirmation and encouragement to them.

Visual |————————————————————————————| Verbal

7. Category: Perspective. The leader is either...
Movement Oriented or Location Oriented

This is very evident in pastors: they will link themselves with the "kingdom" at large (movement) or identify more with their own personal work (church) and geographical location.

Movement |————————————————————————————| Location

8. Category: Ministry Paradigm. The leader is either...
Shepherd or Rancher

These paradigm symbols were popularized by Carl George. He notes that the leader will either insist on doing all the tasks or will withdraw and insist his student leaders do it all.

Shepherd |————————————————————————————| Rancher

9. Category: People Skills. The leader is either...
Tough or Tender

This campus leader is perceived as either a tough-minded confronter or a tender-hearted caregiver. This can help us understand our bent toward policy pushing versus student pleasing.

Tough |————————————————————————————| Tender

10. Category: Excellence. The leader is either...
Performance Driven or Authenticity Driven
Many collegiate leaders either evaluate the success of a program by excellence of performance (good platform, it all ran on time) or by how genuinely it ministered to the students (unpolished platform, but real).

Performance |————————————————————————————————| Authenticity

11. Category: Worship Style. The leader is either...
Celebration Based or Reflection Based
In regard to corporate worship experience, this collegiate leader generally will lean toward a preference toward celebrative praises or reflective worship in the services.

Celebration |————————————————————————————————| Reflection

12. Categories: Values. The leader has either...
Unity Values or Purity Values
The leader values unity (harmony) in the body, sometimes at the expense of principles; or demands purity (doctrinal integrity) among students, often costing relationships and harmony.

Unity |————————————————————————————————| Purity

13. Category: Discipleship. The leader is either...
Classroom Dependent or Coach Dependent
Whether or not he/she admits it, this collegiate leader believes disciples are made from the teaching or preaching in meetings, or from one-to-one relationships (mentoring clusters). Note what you rely on more.

Classroom |————————————————————————————————| Coach

14. Category: Change. The leader is either...
Comfortable with Tradition or Comfortable with Trends
Some collegiate leaders either draw energy from the past, familiar methods, or the latest change in trends. These leaders tend to draw comfort from familiarity or raw change.

Tradition |————————————————————————————————| Trends

Once you're finished, review your marks. Are you an extreme on any of the categories? Learning to function well in each of these categories is a little like walking a tight rope. Leaning too far to one side or the other will throw you off balance. Evaluate yourself.

There is more than one way to lead an organization well.

Coming to Terms...

So what can we conclude from these observations? Since we've concluded collegiate leaders are different, is there anything we can really do about it? Absolutely. The following are my primary conclusions, based upon the information we've just examined:

- No one "right" method has emerged for effective leadership. There is more than one way to lead an organization well.
- We eventually form a natural leadership identity. We should know where our natural strengths exist, and in what contexts we will most likely flourish. We must learn to play to our strengths, as we work on our weaknesses.

We must know
when we cannot
change and when
we must be flexible.

We still use
"scapegoats" today.

- The "means of influence" or leadership style we exercise with a student group must change, depending on the situation. We must determine what is appropriate, and when.
- We must know when we cannot change, and when we must be flexible. There's a need for solid philosophical leadership base, including core values and guiding principles. As leaders, we need to be flexible. We need to take into account various factors oftentimes because of the school we may be working with and define our leadership style accordingly. We need to find balance. Are there times when a leader should not be flexible? Take time to reflect on what you see as the "inflexibles" in leadership.
- We must seek a mature balance in each category of our leadership so that our style does not prevent us from accomplishing our mission.
- We must place complimentary staff and volunteers in appropriate positions so that collegiate leaders are not lost due to our weaknesses. There is no reason why a campus ministry or church cannot be strong and balanced in all categories.

Bringing it All Home

Back in the Old Testament, the Book of Leviticus tells of a sacred custom called the "escaped goat." When the troubles of people became too much, a healthy male goat was brought into the temple. In a solemn ceremony, the highest priest of the tribe placed his hands of the head of the goat and recited the list of woes. The problems were then transferred onto the goat, and the goat was set free, taking the troubles away with him (Lev. 16:21).

Even though that was about 4,000 years ago, we still use "scapegoats" today. We frequently blame other people or other things in our lives to avoid accepting responsibility for who we are and what we do. Instead of working on what is going on inside us, we try to blame that which is around us.

It's always easier and more convenient to assume the answer lies elsewhere. When life gets tough, we start to think, "It's this job." We often use our scapegoat for the wrong stuff circulating inside us. It's time to act, beginning with prayer. Seek the Lord for wisdom concerning your leadership. Is it healthy? What kind of leader did He wire you to be? Where will you flourish for His kingdom? In what areas must you mature and deepen to become all you were intended to be? Are you teachable? What's your plan for personal growth? Will you take the risks and do what you need to do?

Think About It

In the space below, write a brief description speaking to the questions in the paragraph you just read.

William James, the father of modern psychology, said, "Compared to what we ought to be, we are only half awake. As leaders we are making use of only a small part of our physical and mental resources. Stating the thing broadly, the human individual lives far within his limits. He possesses power of various sorts, which he habitually fails to use."

There's a great story about a man who died and met St. Peter at the gates of heaven. Recognizing the saint's knowledge and wisdom, he wanted to ask him a question. "St. Peter," he said, "I have been interested in military history for many years. Tell me, who was the greatest general of all time?"

Peter quickly responded, "Oh, that is a simple question. It's that man right over there."

The man looked where Peter was pointing and answered, "You must be mistaken. I knew that man on earth, and he was a common laborer who didn't really accomplish much."

"That's right," Peter remarked, "but he would have been the greatest general of all time—if he had been a general."

Seek the Lord for wisdom concerning your leadership.

Assessment

What are some conclusions you have drawn about your leadership style? Jot them down in this part of your book. Look upon this as a part of your spiritual journey.

Further Reading

Developing the Leader Within You, John Maxwell, Thomas Nelson Publishers, 2001
Wild at Heart, John Eldredge, Thomas Nelson Publishers, 2001 (for men)
Certain Trumpets, Garry Wills, Simon and Schuster, 1995
The On-Purpose Person, Kevin McCarthy, NavPress, 2001
Nobody in Charge, Harland Cleveland, Wiley, John & Sons, 2002
Living On Purpose, Christine and Tom Sine, Baker Book House, 2002

Charting Your Course

IDENTIFYING YOUR VISION, PLANNING YOUR STRATEGY

"Make Your ways known to me, LORD; teach me Your paths. Guide me in Your truth and teach me, for You are the God of my salvation."
—Psalm 25:4-5 (HCSB®)

"There is in the act of preparing the moment you start caring."
—Winston Churchill

I want you to meet four collegiate workers, each who direct a campus ministry. Perhaps you've met them already.

Sam is impressive. He immediately strikes me as a spiritual giant. He's memorized a lot of Scripture and his prayers are eloquent. If you ever have a Bible question, Sam's the one to go to. He's taken over a campus ministry at the local university and is already talking about how it's going to be different—how it'll grow and reach new students. In fact, he's talking about planting more campus ministries once this one takes off. There's just one glitch. When anyone asks him how he's going to do it, he looks at them in a patronizing way, and says, "God is going to take care of that. I'm living by faith. I'm praying and trusting God for the fruit."

If you were to listen to Sam, you'd instantly feel funny that you even asked such a fleshly question. At the same time, you have this sneaking suspicion that something's wrong. You visit Sam after a couple of years, only to find that nothing has happened. Because Sam is so good at spiritualizing his dreams, he's failed to crystallize any plans to make them happen. He has confused God's role and his own role.

Dan is quite different. He loves God, but is far less apt to talk big talk. In fact, Dan might not talk much vision at all. He's been leading his campus ministry for years, and everyone on campus knows and loves him. That's because he doesn't make ripples. He never rocks the boat. He never stirs the waters. In fact, he doesn't do much of anything outside of protocol. Somewhere in his past, he decided he was going to play defense rather than offense in his ministry. He holds weekly meetings, elects new officers each year, and gives a nice little gift to the graduating seniors in May. But that's it. He just holds the fort down—and never attacks the enemy. He doesn't take any new ground for the kingdom of God. He's never assessed his ministry for strengths and weaknesses. He has no plans to do anything other than what he's always done. He was trained years ago in student ministry, and he's stuck. The problem is, so is his ministry.

Tom is a toxic ministry leader, though you may not see it right away. He's a driver, and at first, he comes across as a natural—a spiritual leader who's determined to do the will of God on his campus. Students are attracted to him because he is so sure of himself and his plans. This guy is going somewhere. The problem is, once you know who he really is, you'd never want to go with him. Tom is pushy and dogmatic. Once he has a plan, he becomes very narrow. He is insensitive to his environment. He uses people to get to his goal and the turnover rate of his student leaders is high. When they leave, he just says they're not very committed. The fact is, no healthy person wants to stay under his leadership. He's never said it, but he could: "It's my way or the highway." He believes he knows how campus ministry works, and he's going to push until he's reached his goal. Just watch out for the wounded people lying in his path.

Vicki is a joy. She leads her campus ministry in the south, and loves it. She is sanguine, and everyone loves being around her. Her personality is magnetic. Wherever she goes, there's a party, and she's the life of that party. Does she have a vision for ministry? You bet she does. The problem is, she's got a new one each week. She's full of vision and ideas, but is mentally scattered. She loves to talk about them and even hear her students' dreams as well. But it's all talk. Nothing is implemented. No one can follow her very well. I'm not sure if she even knows where she's going. Her charisma helps get students to the Bible study. Sadly, there's no depth or game plan for their growth once they come. Vicki's ministry is five miles wide and one inch deep. Her ministry revolves around her personality, not a strategic plan for reaching and discipling students. She'd love to have a plan, but she doesn't know how. She's never equipped a student for ministry or leadership in her life. Vicki has a lot of fun, but not a lot of fruit.

Have you met any of these campus leaders while ministering on a college campus? Have you ever see them in the mirror? It is probable each of us have acted out the stories of Sam, or Dan, or Tom, or Vicki in some season of our lives. When you see them in yourself or in others, you'll notice something very quickly. While all the leaders are different, they have produced ministries that reflect their personalities. Pastor Rick Warren has said, "If you want to know the spiritual temperature of a ministry, put a thermometer in the leader's mouth."

Unfortunately, some campus leaders have failed to impact their campus for Christ. It isn't that they don't want to—they just haven't taken the steps to do so. We'll discuss these steps.

Try This Out...

Review the story of the four campus leaders above. Which one do you most identify with? Why? You may identify with just one aspect of each. What are these? Take a moment and be gut-level honest. Write a brief paragraph that summarizes your own campus leadership, so far.

Now the questions is, how would your students, faculty, church, and others react to your statements? Would they feel you are in touch with your own leadership style? Which box would most likely be identified by those who work with you on the campus?

❏ Yes   ❏ Maybe   ❏ Sometimes   ❏ Hardly ever   ❏ No

In this chapter I hope you can address the areas in which you are weak. My goal isn't to discourage you—quite the opposite. I want to be your ministry's best friend, helping you to assess reality, then lay an appropriate plan to reach your campus.

"If you want to know the spiritual temperature of a ministry, put a thermometer in the leader's mouth."
—Rick Warren

Is It in the Bible?

I have struggled in the past with the seeming paradox of trusting God and making plans. Each time I failed to lay any plans for my ministry, I felt as though I was cheating my students. I was "winging it." And they could tell. On the other hand, when I made plans, I always felt I was somehow quenching God's Spirit, or His desire to do more than my little plans could accommodate. I had obviously drifted into the flesh, or so I thought.

It was encouraging to me to study how much planning is mentioned in the Bible. It is safe to say it's a God thing. We can plan under the inspiration of the Holy Spirit just as we can minister under His inspiration. Our goal should be to align ourselves with the plans of God, and move with Him. Organizing any size group of students requires you to make some plans beforehand. Notice how God is the Master Planner:

> "Have you not heard? I designed it long ago;
> I planned it in days gone by. I have now brought it to pass"
> (Isa. 37:26, HCSB®).

> " 'I know the plans I have for you,' says the LORD,
> 'wholesome plans and not harmful,
> to give you a future and hope' " (Jer. 29:11, HCSB®).

God's not the only One either. He called several leaders to partner with Him, and to lay plans in the process. He actually used their planning to further His plans for the world. For instance, Noah received explicit instructions from God to build the ark. God gave detailed measurements to Noah, who was faithful to carry out the long-range plan. He finished the ark's construction exactly as God told him—in 120 years! It was built so well that it withstood 40 days of torrential rain, then floated a solid year as the floods subsided (Gen. 7-9).

The long-range plan of Nehemiah was to see the wall of Jerusalem rebuilt. He visualized the completion of the wall, then began his plans for its construction. His story is a wonderful picture of God's providence coupled with man's preparation. It was a combo of God's favor and Nehemiah's faithfulness. The work was completed in 52 days because each family was assigned a certain portion of the wall to build. Nehemiah planned and organized the project with excellence (Neh. 1-5).

The long-range plan of David was to build the temple (2 Sam. 7). God did not allow David to build it because of his association with wars (2 Kings 5:2-3). However, when Solomon was chosen to succeed him, David handed Solomon the completed plan for the temple and a list of materials on hand. After seven years of construction, the temple was completed, and the long-range plan of David was fulfilled.

Unless we study the Scripture closely, we may fail to notice that Jesus frequently spoke about the necessity of planning and strategy. In fact, in two of His parables Jesus told stories about how foolish it was to neglect planning. Read each passage of Scripture and see what it has to say about planning.

- The Wise and Foolish Builders (Matt. 7:24-27)
- The Builder Counting the Cost (Luke 14:28-30)
- The King Planning for Battle (Luke 14:31-32)
- The Unjust Steward (Luke 16:1-8)

God is the Master Planner.

Four Crucial Steps

Authors in corporate America have written material on the subject of planning and organizational change. Men such as Peter Senge, John Kotter, and Jim Collins suggest some helpful steps for all leaders who want to improve their organization. Joe Graham, state director for Georgia Baptist Collegiate Ministries, has taken four crucial steps and applied them to campus ministry. Let's spend the rest of this chapter walking through these important steps:

- Assess
- Envision
- Design
- Implement

Assess

I've been privileged to visit England five times. Each time I'm in London, I enjoy using the subway system that the locals affectionately call "the tube." I can still hear the pre-recorded message that spouts off each time the subway doors open on the railcars. A synthesized voice says, "Mind the gap" meaning, "Watch your step, because there is a gap between the platform and the railcar."

Most campus leaders need a voice giving the same message to them each year. We must "mind the gap" between our present reality and the vision we possess for our ministry. Good leaders are always aware of how wide that gap is. They know because they consistently perform an assessment on their ministry. They're not afraid to face the music and discover where they're weak. Author Max Dupree has said many times: "The first job of the leader is to define reality." This job requires evaluation.

In his book, *The Fifth Discipline,* Peter Senge refers to this gap, as a "creative tension" and likens it to a rubber band being stretched. One end of the rubber band represents reality, as you know it in your ministry today. The other end symbolizes your vision. As you stretch the rubber band it creates a tension between your reality and your vision.[1] The tension you experience can include pressures, frustrations, occasional failures, and even anxiety. Sometimes you'll ask yourself silently, *"Is this all there is to my ministry? Does it get any better?"* Noah must have asked these questions as he built an ark in dry heat. Jeremiah must have asked them as he continued to preach to Israel, waiting years for anyone to respond to his message. Ninety-year-old Abraham must have asked them as he waited a decade for his son to be born. Job must have asked them as he sat around with boils all over his body, listening to criticism, waiting for God to bring justice to his life. It's tough to mind the gap, but good leaders do it.

So what should you assess? Are there certain areas you must evaluate on a regular basis? Absolutely! Let me suggest a handful of issues every organizational leader should assess at least once a year. The all-encompassing question you must answer is: *Does my ministry have a healthy culture or a toxic culture?*

Mark on the chart where you think your ministry would fall today.

Continuum

Toxic 1——-2——-3——-4——-5——-6——-7——-8——-9——-10 Healthy

Remember: Healthy things naturally grow. Toxic environments create stagnation and destruction. What score would you like to give your campus ministry today?

Following are the central issues I believe you must assess in your ministry on campus. Take a moment and reflect, then give yourself as honest an answer as you can for each question.

"The first job of the leader is to define reality."
—Max Dupree

It's tough to mind the gap, but good leaders do it.

There are, in fact,
many leadership styles
that work, both in the
marketplace and in
the ministry.

Vision
1. Would the average student in our ministry say that our vision is crystal clear?
2. Do our students know how they can participate in some way to accomplish the vision?

Communication
1. Do our students and staff in our ministry experience open and honest communication?
2. Do those in our ministry feel free to express their thoughts and feelings with one another?

Leadership Development
1. Do we have a system that equips students in leadership?
2. Does our ministry value leadership and help potential leaders to naturally develop?

Values
1. Do students and others who work with us know the core values of our ministry?
2. Do those who serve in our ministry incarnate our core values?

Structure
1. Have we established a structure that develops students and other leaders to their potential?
2. Does our structure hinder or accelerate the mission of our ministry to college students?

Fundamentals
1. Evangelism: How do we cast vision, equip, and sponsor outreach on our campus/church to reach students on a daily and weekly basis?
2. Bible Study: How do we enable students to "squeeze their own juice" in the Scriptures as we have structured Bible study?
3. Worship: How do we foster a worship experience that leads to intimacy with God?
4. Discipleship: How do we mentor believers to know God, their identity, and mission?
5. Fellowship: How do we encourage community where students can share life together?
6. Service: How do we create opportunities for students to discover and use their gifts?
7. Leadership: How do we empower students to lead others effectively?

Is That Your Final Answer?

I suggest you answer the questions listed above with a key group of students/adults in your ministry. Don't just settle for the first answer that surfaces. Talk them over, dig for details, and try to answer why things are the way they are. Then be ready to talk over the necessary steps you'll need to take in order to change. You may want to end by looking at your SWOT: Strengths, Weaknesses, Opportunities, and Threats. This should spark good discussion.

Before you are finished, take a stab at these big-picture questions with your team:

1. Does our ministry place a high priority on our values and our ultimate mission?
2. How is this priority demonstrated? How do we invest time and resources in light of it?
3. Is there some aspect of our organization's culture that is hindering the mission?
4. What are the basic assumptions by which our ministry operates?
5. How is conflict handled in our organization?
6. How are influence, power, and authority distributed in our organization?
7. What level of participation exists in our ministry?

Dr. Ignaz Semmelweis was a surgeon who delivered babies at Vienna's General Hospital in the mid-1800s. A problem in his section of the maternity ward consumed him. The mortality rate of mothers was sky-high. One out of every 10 women died during the birthing process.

Your mission should be birthed out of your vision. Vision is what you see. Mission is what you *do* about it.

If it's time for you to give birth to a new vision, keep in mind that God is the source of it. While there is such a thing as a "man-made vision," I don't think you or I want to be part of something less than what God creates. Your mission should be birthed out of your vision. Vision is what you see. Mission is what you *do* about it. So before you start out on your mission you need to ask yourself: what's my vision?

I have found God-given visions are born much like babies are born. It's a process. It doesn't happen overnight. Consider this process and the following stages.

Intimacy—*This is the place of beginnings. People who catch a vision do so because they have spent time in quietness, solitude, and reflection. Just as a husband and wife won't give birth to a baby unless they experience intimacy, you will never receive a vision from God unless you experience intimacy with Him. Give Him a chance to speak to you.*

Conception—*At times during this reflection, a vision is conceived. Just as a husband and wife don't get pregnant every time they come together, so God doesn't drop a vision on you each time you worship Him. However, there are times when He will plant the seed of a vision in you. Often, God provides it in infant form. It may still be fuzzy, without all of the details, but it is forming inside. In the same way a baby looks like both Mom and Dad, so your vision will look like both God and you (It fits your passion.).*

Gestation—*This period of time is often the longest stage of the process. During this time the leader identifies with the problem, intercedes for the campus, and intervenes in the process. I suggest you prayer walk, observing different parts of the campus as you wander and pray. As your vision grows, it enlarges you, just like a child in the womb transforms its mom. This stage is the one in which we are most tempted to abort the vision.*

As your vision grows, it enlarges you.

Labor—*This stage is often the most painful. Just as birth pains increase in intensity and frequency, so the fight intensifies just before the vision is fulfilled. The enemy would like nothing more than to entice you to throw in the towel and quit, just before the vision is born. Labor is a good sign that something is about to happen!*

Birth—*Finally the vision is born. All that has been going on inside the heart of you as the leader is ultimately realized. Everyone can now see the fruit of the prayer, planning, and work. As in first viewing your newborn, you feel like your vision is the most beautiful one of all. Warning: others may want to celebrate with you at this point, and you will wonder where they were during all the labor! Let it go. Celebrate together, then get ready to parent that vision until it matures! By the way, your vision will leave stretch marks on you. You'll never be satisfied with a man-made vision again.*

As you consider the vision God might have for you, keep in mind that your personal vision should overlap with your ministry's vision. Ideally, they're one and the same. God may speak to you through several voices:

- The Inward Voice: What's your passion? What fires you up and gives you conviction?
- The Unhappy Voice: What are your burdens? What makes you cry or makes you angry?
- The Outward Voice: What do Christian friends confirm about you and your calling?
- The Strong Voice: What are your primary spiritual gifts, natural talents, and acquired skills?
- The Soothing Voice: What area of ministry is most fulfilling to you when you do it?
- The Fruitful Voice: What gives you the greatest results when you do it?

Now apply these ideas to the fundamentals as you continue to develop your ministry. Think about your vision and mission in each of the big seven areas:

EVANGELISM
What do you see?
What will you do?

SERVICE
What do you see?
What will you do?

WORSHIP
What do you see?
What will you do?

BIBLE STUDY
What do you see?
What will you do?

DISCIPLESHIP
What do you see?
What will you do?

LEADERSHIP DEVELOPMENT
What do you see?
What will you do?

FELLOWSHIP
What do you see?
What will you do?

Design

This step of the process is critical, but must follow assessment and envisioning. Don't ever come up with a plan without first taking time to evaluate and envision. In one sense, the first step is about burden. Burdens happen when you see things as they are. Vision happens when you see things as God wants them to be. Once you can see what God would like to do, the next step is to co-labor with Him as you design an action plan.

I have a friend named Noble Bowman. He's been a campus minister at the University of Central Arkansas for years. His ministry has grown, spiritually and numerically, but only because he has walked through the process of assessment, envision, and design. Only a couple of dozen students came to his first meeting. This wasn't bad. He just knew God wanted to do so much more on the UCA campus. After months of doing status quo ministry, Noble decided to meet with his top 10 "core" students and assess the ministry. He called it a "hard-core" evaluation. Nothing was sacred; anything that wasn't of God or wasn't fruitful would be scrapped. They determined that their main meeting needed changes; they didn't do small groups very effectively and they weren't discipling students or equipping leaders well. (Hmmm. Other than that, everything was great!)

They prayed intensely, then asked the question: what could happen in the next five years if we didn't have limitations of people or money? They began to think about five years down the road. This was huge—those students were envisioning long-term, after each of them would graduate. Then they began to list what they would need to do over the next year if that vision were to be reached. They set one-semester goals, one-year goals, and two-year goals. They committed it all to paper. Finally they began to devise a plan. They set goals for each area that needed changes.

Nobel told me five years later that he began to rummage through his files. He came upon that original page where they had written their vision and their plans to reach their specific goals. He had to smile. They had reached every one of them.

Jesus Touched Him Again

You may remember the story of Jesus healing a blind man in Mark 8:22-26. He touched the man, then asked if he could see. The man said he could, but that he saw people as trees walking about. In other words, his vision was partially there—he wasn't blind. But there was still

Burdens happen when you see things as they are.

Vision happens when you see things as God wants them to be.

some impairment. We don't know if the man was nearsighted, farsighted, or if he had astigmatism. In any case—Jesus touched him again and his vision was clear.

Jesus touched him again, and his vision was clear.

Let's apply this to us today. You may feel like that man—you can see, but your vision is unclear. Many collegiate leaders suffer from a lack of spiritual vision. Their problem is usually one of three options:

- Nearsightedness: They only see their own local, immediate work—nothing outside the box.
- Farsightedness: They only see some lofty, far-away target, but can't translate it into action.
- Astigmatism: They have an inability to focus.

Do you suffer from any of these? If so, you may need Jesus to touch you again. Ask Him to help you out of whatever box you are in. Ask Him to clarify your vision to implement your design.

Four Types of Planning

As you design a structure for your ministry, you'll need to do four types of planning. In the table below, note how planning moves from left to right; from big to little picture.

	CONCEPTUAL	STRATEGIC	LONG-TERM	OPERATIONAL
Who:	You	Few	Few	Everyone
Issue:	Dreams	Clear vision	Ideas	Objectives
Outcome:	Philosophy	Approach	Results	Tasks
Timing:	Futuristic	5-10 years out	3-5 years out	1 year out
Answers:	Why?	Why?	How?	How? When?
Nature:	No limits; what you can imagine	The end is in mind; starts at your goal	Starts where you are right now	Determines short-range direction

Ask God to clarify your vision of ministry on the campus.

A Structure for Design

Think about it. If a building is under construction on your campus, who has more influence on its look and function than anyone else? The architect. In ministry, it's the same story. Let's say you were to start from scratch with your ministry on campus—clean slate. Once you know your vision and your values, you can begin to form a structure to accomplish your vision and values. If you truly desire to host a ministry that reflects the heart of Jesus, then your focus in all of your events should be on honoring God. The activity in all of your events will revolve around developing people. Put simply…

Your Focus: Honor God
Your Method: Develop People

In the next chapter, we will focus entirely on establishing a structure that accomplishes this focus and method. For now, let me suggest a simple "funnel" that diagrams how you might place each of the activities in your ministry:

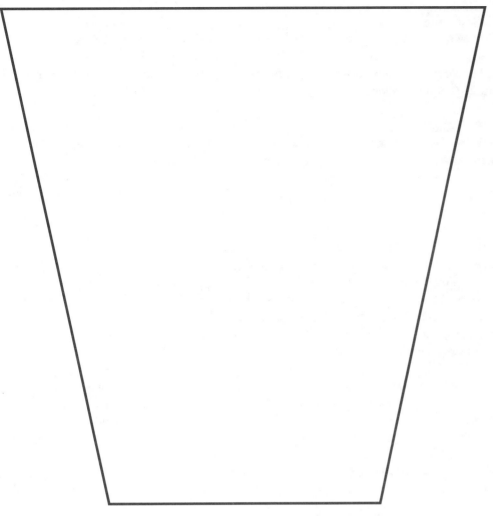

As you plan your ministry, you may want to add each level as you go down the funnel. I use a funnel diagram because fewer students participate as you move down the funnel. Once you train a core group of initial leaders and assemble a list of potential group members, begin at the top of the funnel with a rally point; then add small groups, and so on. Read and reflect on the next chapter carefully as we go in-depth on design and structure.

Implement

The final step leaders must take is to implement the vision. Planning only helps if we are committed to implementation. Let me suggest the following steps as you implement:

1. Plan to Plan

It is important to understand that one must plan to plan. A certain amount of time and energy must be allotted in the weekly agenda for this process. This is the number-one mistake made in ministries. Everyone agrees strategic planning is important, but they fail to plan to plan.

A Planning and Work Ratio

Plan	Execute	
		= **X Results**

Plan	Execute	
		= **X Results**

Once you train a core group of initial leaders and assemble a list of potential group members, begin at the top of the funnel with a rally point, then add small groups, and so on.

It is important to understand that one must plan to plan.

2. Determine Your Primary Purpose

Sit down and decide why you exist. Discuss this with key leaders in your life and ministry. What is your reason for being—your mission? Earlier, we discussed four types of planning. After completing conceptual planning, purposeful ministries do two more types of planning: strategic and operational.

3. Assess the Situation

We covered assessment earlier. This is where it best fits. Before you implement any plan you must evaluate. Strategy is first trying to understand where you fit in today's world. It's not about where you wish you were or where you hoped you would be, but where you are. Then it's trying to understand where you want to be five years out. Finally, it's assessing the realistic changes of getting from here to there.

4. Prioritize the Needs

Make sure your collegiate team agrees on what goals are most important. As a team, list them in the order of importance and priority. Then stick to them. Don't deviate or become distracted by anything. Do you remember the analogy of the rocks and the jars? A man once stood in front of an audience with two jars and a bunch of rocks. He began to fill one jar arbitrarily with small rocks, medium-sized rocks, and big ones. Soon it was full and there were several rocks left over that didn't fit.

He said: "Let's imagine this jar represents your week. The big rocks represent important goals, the little ones less important goals. Your schedule is so full, you can't fit everything in. Consequently, some of the more important actions never happen." Then he took the second jar and said: "Let's put in the big rocks first, then see if there is room for the others." As he did so, it was apparent the strategy worked. Once the big rocks were in, the other smaller ones fit easily, as they slipped down through the crevices. The goal, he said, is to make sure you put the big rocks in first. The issue is not prioritizing your schedule, but rather scheduling your priorities.

5. Ask the Right Questions

MARKET: Who are we trying to serve and what needs are we meeting?
LEADERSHIP: Do we have the right people at the top to accomplish our goals?
COUNSEL: Whose advice do we need in order to succeed?
DIRECTION: Exactly what are we going to do short-, mid-, and long-range?
ORGANIZATION: Who's responsible for what? Who will supervise whom?
CASH: What are our expected expenses and income?
REPORTING: Are we on target?
COMMUNICATION: How can we effectively make known what we're doing?
EVALUATING: Are we seeking the quality we expect from ourselves?
REFINING: How can we keep improving in the critical aspects of this ministry?

6. Set Specific Goals

In order for a goal to be reached, it must conform to the following criteria. It must be...

Written	Measurable
Specific	Personal
Realistic	Convictional

7. Clarify and Communicate

How often have you sat through a productive planning session, left the meeting enthused about results, yet nothing ever materialized? There is a specific link between planning and implementation: the link is clarification and communication.

Put the big rocks in first.

There is a specific link between planning and implementation: the link is clarification and communication.

Each Planning Meeting Should Include:

A written conclusion   A listing of resources
Individuals' responsibility   Next steps
Time line   The person in charge of the project

8. Identify Possible Obstacles
At this step you are actually doing negative thinking. Think of obstacles that might occur so you can develop ways to overcome them. Imagine a "worst-case scenario" and how you can keep it under control.
   a. The most important prerequisite before implementing a plan: "The Mental Walk-Through"
   b. The most important result of any planning meeting: "The Next Steps"

9. Have an Open-System Approach in Your Planning
An open system is sympathetic to its environment; it allows external entities to influence the decision-making and planning process. A closed system attempts to exist with no regard to concerns outside itself. Our world changes too fast for our ministries not to be flexible. Mission never changes; methods may constantly change.

10. Schedule and Budget
Put your items on a schedule that is responsible yet productive. Without a schedule you can't keep on track. Budget is closely tied to schedule. You must determine the cost of the project or ministry and at what point those costs will be incurred. As much as possible, attempt to remove any surprises.

11. Monitor and Correct
The life of an organization moving through time is like a canoe trip on a large river. Regardless of how conscientiously plans are made, there is a constant need for monitoring and correction if the final destination is to be reached. This should be done often with students/faculty/administrators/other adults assisting in ministry.

12. Go Public with Your Ministry
It's important to take the time to communicate with other ministries and churches what your ministry is doing. Sharing our vision and fund-raising are often at the bottom of our "to do" list, but they are crucial. You don't serve in a vacuum. Churches/campus programs can help you with funding and with communicating your vision to others if you build relationships, add value to them, and keep them posted on what's happening. Plan a time to go to churches or to the director of campus ministries, both to give them something (add value to them) and to share what you are doing.

Study the Results

Once you've done all twelve steps (and you will feel like you've been through a twelve-step program!) you must watch outcomes. "Keeping score" is the only way to know if you're winning or losing. Develop vehicles to keep score. If you're going to make change, you should do it off of current information. As you discover what's happening, saturate your ministry in prayer. This is where God's providence and your preparation come together.

"No wisdom, no understanding, and no counsel [will prevail] against the LORD.
A horse is prepared for the day of battle,
but victory comes from the LORD" (Prov. 21:30-31, HCSB®)

Mission never changes; methods may constantly change.

Assessment

Guide your key leaders in your collegiate program to identify your ministry's strengths and weaknesses in each of the areas of:

- Assess
- Envision
- Design
- Implement

Individually do the exercises in this chapter for each topic.

Set a date to come together with your leadership and corporately discuss your answers. Take this opportunity to hear everyone's perspective on where your campus ministry is positioned currently. Then take the next steps to strengthen the weaknesses and move forward to fulfill your vision.

Further Reading

Visioneering, Andy Stanley, Multnomah Publishers, 2001
The Fifth Discipline, Peter Senge, Doubleday & Company, 1994
Leaders Everywhere, Tim Elmore and Art Fuller, Growing Leaders, 2002
Good to Great, Jim Collins, Harper Information, 2001
The Master Plan of Evangelism, Robert Coleman, Fleming H. Revell, 1994
Generating Hope: A Strategy for Reaching The Postmodern Generation, Jimmy Long, InterVarsity Press, 1997

Drawing Lines and Writing Stories

MINISTRY STRUCTURES THAT DEVELOP PEOPLE

"And He personally gave some to be apostles, some prophets, some evangelists, some pastors and teachers, for the training of the saints in the work of ministry, to build up the body of Christ."
—*Ephesians 4:11-12 (HCSB®)*

"It is only in developing people that we permanently succeed."
—*Harvey Firestone*

Many churches and campus ministries today labor under the notion that genuine renewal will occur in their ministries via some mystical, supernatural movement of God. They are not committed to making disciples or equipping people, as the New Testament teaches. Instead, they are hopeful that someday God will sovereignly move among them during a Bible study, and folks will somehow mature. It is an unpredictable, subjective, and even mysterious outcome.

It's easy to excuse our complacency and disobedience to the fundamentals by saying that God is the Source of all genuine transformation. The truth is, God is indeed the Source, but He generally never works alone. History teaches us that He is consistently at work in those who practice the art of developing people. If revival is what we desire—if we're to lead people to experience God's best for them—we must return to the biblical art of developing people.

> Jesus was intentional about developing people.

What Would Jesus Do?

It is safe to say that Jesus was intentional about developing people. Note His methodology for "world conquest" during His three-and-a-half-year ministry.

- He stayed up all night praying for the selection of 12 men to develop.
- He spent the majority of His time with those 12 disciples.
- His method for making disciples was mentoring.
- Even His ministry to the masses was a model to train His disciples.
- He fully expected them to reproduce what He had done when He left them.
- The early church reached entire cities and nations because they were committed to this practice of developing and discipling people (Acts 17:6; 19:10).

Jesus' Paradigm for Developing People

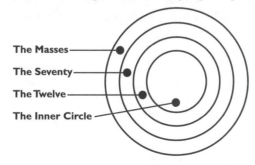

The Masses
The Seventy
The Twelve
The Inner Circle

I believe Jesus intentionally fostered the relationships He experienced with people. In fact, I believe there were at least four circles of influence He had with people, as you see in the diagram. He challenged them to move from an outer circle to an inner circle of intimacy with Him and commitment to God. Do you remember His words to the small group of men who did make that move? Jesus said, "I do not call you slaves anymore, because a slave doesn't know what his master is doing. I have called you friends, because I have made known to you everything I have heard from My Father" (John 15:15, HCSB®).

His 12 were faithful to reproduce precisely what He'd taught them. The apostle John, for instance, discipled (or mentored) Polycarp—a man who carried the legacy well into the second century. In fact, the art of disciple-making or equipping people through developmental relationships continued strong through the third century before it was dealt a horrible blow in A.D. 313. Ironically, the "blow" came from the Emperor Constantine, a confessed Christian man. It was during that year Constantine declared Christianity as the "state" religion. All of a sudden, God's people moved from being persecuted outcasts to being part of the system. They were vogue. Instantly, everyone was declared a Christian. Outreach no longer seemed necessary. They began to withdraw from their labor of discipling people. Unfortunately, it was when God's people stopped developing others that the renewal began to fade as well. Following this period, the church of Jesus Christ became institutionalized. Slowly, it became more of a cold, stained-glass monument, rather than a living organism that was on the move, developing and mentoring others in their intimacy with God.

> Success without a successor is a failure.

History Repeats Itself

Time and time again, history has told the same story. During the 18th century under the direction of John Wesley, a movement began called Methodism. Note some of the highlights:
- Wesley took the gospel outside the four walls of the church.
- Wesley realized that decisions don't automatically equal disciples.
- Wesley organized converts into class meetings for accountability and growth.
- Wesley began to develop and mentor lay ministers who served the church.
- Wesley built chapels for the purpose of equipping lay people for ministry.
- Wesley believed all should be unleashed to minister and reach their potential.

John Wesley was committed to two tasks that his church would later neglect.

First, he was committed to putting the truths and values of his movement on paper. His writings on sanctification, personal growth, discipline, and evangelism are still influencing us today.

Second, he was committed to training a second generation of men to lead when he was gone. He somehow knew that success without a successor is a failure.

Try This Out!

Take a moment and reflect on your collegiate ministry. In what areas are you truly committed to the art of developing students and others on the campus and equipping them for spiritual reproduction? Jot down at least three in the space provided.

The Lies We Believe

We must face the facts. The reason students and other adults aren't prepared for leadership in the church or on campus is because present leaders have failed to equip them. Further, leaders have failed because they have unwittingly bought into one of a series of "myths" about leadership. Listed below are some popular myths.

1. **The Transfer Myth**—*These campus workers believe that leaders will transfer to them from other churches or colleges.*
2. **The Bird-in-the-Hand Myth**—*These campus workers are only concerned with "plugging holes" and they have enough leaders now.*
3. **The Irreplaceability Myth**—*You may feel that no one can ever do the leadership thing quite as well as you do.*
4. **The Short-Sighted Myth**—*These campus workers don't see the future very clearly and the need for more leaders tomorrow.*
5. **The Inferiority Myth**—*Perhaps you quietly fear there may be a better leader who will emerge from the students or other adults.*
6. **The "Easier-to-Do-It-Myself" Myth**—*We're too busy already. It will require too much work to set up the training necessary.*
7. **The Reproduction Myth**—*Despite our own lack of leadership training, we assume we'll reproduce spiritual leaders on campus naturally.*
8. **The Theology Myth**—*We think collegiate leaders will arise out of thin air since God is sovereign.*

Question: *Have you bought into any of these myths?*   ❑ *Yes*   ❑ *At times*   ❑ *No*

If you answered "Yes" or "At times," how will you combat them?

Drawing Lines, Writing Stories

As we have already concluded, equipping or developing people is a process, not an event. It includes instruction, demonstration, experience, and assessment of progress on a consistent basis. However, it begins when the pastor or campus minister practices an art that I call "drawing lines and writing stories." This process will create a structure for ongoing student/leader development on your campus.

1. Determine the STORY you want to write through your college ministry.
Every church or campus ministry is writing a story—whether or not they realize it. We write them by accident or on purpose. When we are not intentional, we decrease our chances at making an impact on our community. We must begin with the end in mind. A leader must ask himself or herself the question: *What do I envision students saying about this church or campus decades from now?* While considering the divine "story" the campus ministry is to write, the leader must look at these factors:
- The Lord—What is God saying to you about your role in His worldwide plan with students?
- The Leader—What are your passions and gifts? What do you bring to the table?
- The Lay (student) Leaders—What contribution fits the people God gave you?
- The Location—What opportunities lie in front of you that may direct your course?
- The Landmarks—What destiny markers are sprinkled over your campus' history?
- The Legacy—Finally, what is it you'd ultimately like to have said about your church/campus ministry with collegians?

2. Establish the DECISIONS people should make in the "story."
People who make progress in their spiritual journey make key decisions along the way. These decisions often serve as "breakthrough" points where they take major steps forward.

> Developing people is a process, not an event.

What do I envision people saying about this church or campus decades from now?

However, while most churches and campuses love to see people make these growth decisions, they don't know how to facilitate them. Many campuses and churches play a cruel "hide and seek" game with their collegiate leadership. They preach that people ought to become "disciples" but don't offer a process to facilitate that outcome. Ask yourself:

- *What decisions do we want to see students make while they are here in the program on the campus and in the church?*
- *How do we facilitate students making these decisions?*

3. Recognize the natural STAGES of growth.

There are obvious stages that people experience as they grow into leaders within the organization. As the pastor or campus minister recognizes them, he or she must set up "laboratories" for people to experiment at that level. The "funnel" diagram below outlines these stages in a church setting.

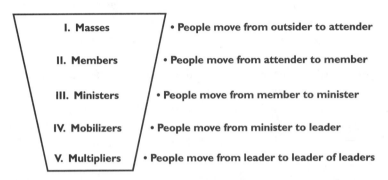

In a campus setting, emerging student leaders also grow through five similar stages. The campus minister can facilitate growth by providing certain activities at each of these levels. These stages and activities are shown in the "funnel" diagram below.

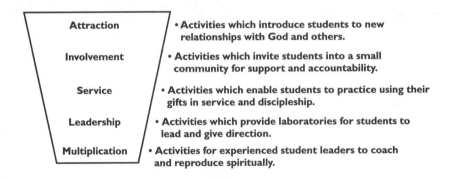

Each stage is a "fishing pool" for the next stage of the process.

Tips on Helping Students Through the Stages...
   a. Each stage represents a relationship and perspective students possess of your ministry.
   b. Each stage is a "fishing pool" for the next stage of the process.
   c. Each stage requires an event students can participate in that helps them grow.
   d. Students must progress through each of these stages sequentially, as a rule.

Question: *As you review the funnel, have you created ministry activities that enable a student to experience growth at each level?* Take a sheet of paper and list the activities and programs.

4. Draw LINES in the sand and help your people cross them.

You've probably heard stories of people who, in a moment of confrontation, take some object, and draw a line in the sand—then challenge their foe to step over that line. In campus ministry students are not foes, but they eventually need a leader who will challenge them to cross a line spiritually.

56 · LEVERAGING YOUR INFLUENCE

At this point, a university pastor or campus minister must begin drawing lines in the sand, and challenge the students and collegiate leaders to take clear steps of commitment that will move them into deeper relationship with God and the organization. Many leaders fear drawing these "lines." They hesitate for fear that no one will ever take the step. The truth is, some will and some won't. But leaders must recognize this reality: they'll never know where your students and other leaders really stand until you draw a line in the sand.

Question: *Can you define those lines in the sand for you as a leader with collegians?*

Some examples of the "lines" you might have to draw include:

- The Ownership Line
  Challenge students and collegiate workers to "own" the vision, and become a part of it. Ask them to become accountable to it.
- The Stewardship Line
  Challenge students and collegiate workers to steward their resources of time, talent, and tithe to further the vision. Ask them to step into ministry.
- The Leadership Line
  Challenge students and collegiate workers to assume a place of influence, and intentionally oversee a segment of students or student leaders in the "story."
- The Authorship Line
  Challenge students and collegiate workers not only to "own the story," but become a key "writer" or multiplier of that story.

<u>5. Create a STRUCTURE for developing people.</u>
All good collegiate leadership development systems begin as "student-development" systems. You don't produce good collegiate leaders unless you first commit to grow them in their beginning stages of your story. The structure must always include spiritual formation. You will eventually turn out leaders as students have grown. Of course, not everyone becomes a formal leader. However, everyone does find their "place" of service where they fit best.

A campus or church's structure for collegiate development must address their different levels of maturity. For example, a pastor could offer four levels of training/ministry experience to people who are ready to take a further step in their involvement. These levels recognize the "stations" where people stop as they mature; they provide a place for everyone, and also a "pool" for you to fish from as you recruit for the next level. They help meet your need to identify people who are ready for deeper involvement.

For example…

Level One: Orientation (Monthly)—This level addresses those who are simply "attenders" but not yet "belongers." Its purpose is to welcome students, to create an atmosphere and climate for growth, to relay the basics in spiritual life, and to communicate to them the goals and opportunities for involvement in your ministry. One-to-one appointments could be set following the orientation event. Greater involvement in church or campus life is seen as a benefit. Those who come to orientation cross an emotional line, and start calling the ministry "their" ministry, not someone else's.

Level Two: Ministry Lifestyle Training (M.L.T.) (Quarterly)—This level addresses those who "own" the vision, but are not serving in ministry. (I trust you embrace the New Testament paradigm that every Christian is called to be a minister.) This is addressed in our first book in this series, *Authentic Influence: Leading Without Titles.* Consequently, the college leader owes it to students to equip them for this task. M.L.T. could be an eight-week training experience where issues are covered like matching gifts and people, the attitude and identity of a minister, people skills, ministry disciplines, and so forth. In this stage, the campus is

All good leadership development systems begin as "student-development" systems.

seen as a "laboratory" for students to experiment in using their gifts in service. They cross a tangible line of involvement, and no longer see themselves as mere "consumers"—they are ministers now.

Level Three: Basic Leadership Training (B.L.T.) (Quarterly)—This level addresses those who are involved in service, but have undeveloped leadership potential. The training will turn "ministers" into "leaders," and provide people who do not simply do the work but oversee the workers. The more leaders a church has, the more growth potential it possesses, and the greater opportunity it has to reach the surrounding community. The more leaders you have in your campus program, the greater your chances of reaching the student body. In this training experience (which could also be done in eight weeks), only those with appropriate leadership gifts move forward. You should not frustrate people without any desire for leadership, and force them to become leaders. B.L.T. serves a vital function, but you should not expect everyone to go through it. B.L.T. might cover such issues as leadership versus ministry, the disciplines of a leader, leadership skills, the anatomy of a leader, and so forth. Many of these issues are addressed in our second book in the series, *Wired for Influence: Skills to Lead Others*. You then move as Moses did (Ex. 18), and place those who've gone through B.L.T. in appropriate leadership positions.

Level Four: "Oasis" (Monthly or Quarterly)—This level serves those already in leadership, and provides ongoing development on a monthly or quarterly basis. It resources collegiate leaders with a time for communication, mutual prayer, encouragement through shared victories, and an opportunity for further training and development. Optimally, it includes a plenary time for all leaders—then, specialty sessions for leaders with and without experience (Foundations and Fitness). For example, you might offer a two-level program such as:
Leadership Foundations: training for those who've been leaders less than a year.
Leadership Fitness: roundtable for those who've been leaders more than one year.

The issues covered in each of the specialty training times (Foundations and Fitness) should be appropriate for collegians and adults who attend them. Leadership Foundations, for instance, would cover fundamentals new leaders need to know, such as servant leadership, communication skills, priorities, conflict resolution, managing people, and so forth. Leadership Fitness is more of a roundtable discussion, allowing experienced leaders to remain on the cutting edge, sharpening their skills in leadership. Issues they might discuss would be: overcoming burnout, mentoring and spiritual reproduction, discipline and confrontation, spiritual passion, effective recruitment, leaders as intercessors, and so on. Another book that might assist you for this level would be our third book, *Intentional Influence: Changing the Campus One Person at a Time*.

Growth Stage	Activity Level	Training to Help Them Progress
Outsider to attender	Attraction	Orientation
Attender to member	Involvement	M.L.T.
Member to minister	Service	B.L.T.
Minister to leader	Leadership	Oasis
Leader of leaders	Multiplication	Personal coaching

Every Christian is called to be a minister.

6. Measure the structure by the QUALITY and QUANTITY of leaders you develop.

As a college leader, your goal is to produce more and better disciples/leaders. If your system is effective, the number of leaders in campus ministry should visibly increase within a year or two. In other words, the system should begin producing a "pool" of leaders to draw from for church and campus positions. If a collegiate, student pastor, campus minister observes that leaders are coming out of the system, he probably is doing a good job at all of the levels of people development. The objectives for your leadership can be drawn up in simple terms:

GOAL #1: To make more and better disciples of Jesus.

GOAL #2: To build more and better leaders of people.

QUANTITY QUESTION: *Are your student leaders more numerous now than in the past?*

QUALITY QUESTION: *Are your student leaders better trained and equipped to be equippers now than in the past?*

The Leader's Personal Evaluation
- Choose the Men/Women
  How creative am I at finding new students and other adults to invest in?
- Cultivate the Models
  How am I doing at turning my students into examples?
- Create the Ministries
  How am I at creating ministry opportunities for them?
- Construct the Management
  How am I at monitoring spiritual progress along the way?
- Communicate the Mindset
  How am I at constantly keeping the vision alive with students and others?
- Celebrate the Mentoring
  How do I encourage and celebrate growth within my program?

Each spring break the campus director at Louisiana State University takes about 250 students to Mexico. This ministry is used as an enlistment tool. The director starts talking about the trip in the fall and begins the sign-up process. The months that follow are preparation months, with incentive for students to prepare spiritually. The director uses international students as translators—many of them making professions of faith along the way! This ministry sparks the growth of student leaders.

At the campus of Southern Mississippi, the BSU director leads a large ministry that uses four leadership teams. Responsibilities are divided among the teams. To attract new students into the process, they host a Big Survival Weekend in September. Because they have so many new students, they hold one event for freshmen and another for the large transfer population. This student-led ministry works because the BSU director has set them up for success by reading his situation so accurately.

The bottom line? If you are going to raise up workers and leaders, you've got to have a plan!

7. Make ADJUSTMENTS each year to maintain progress.

Change is necessary. If it works today, we cannot assume it will again tomorrow. A collegiate program in the church or on campus will either evaluate or stagnate. There must be continual improvement. Collegiate leaders must strive to stay ahead of the game, especially in the area of leader development. Growth and change are topics that have been studied for years. Today, however, growth and change take place at a much faster rate than ever before in recorded history. British author Charles Handy popularized the "Sigmoid Curve" in his attempt to explain and exhort leaders/managers regarding corporate change. Note the following diagram.

> A collegiate ministry will either evaluate or stagnate.

Change at Points A and B...

Organizations and ministries grow in a fashion similar to the arrow in the diagram to the right. When the arrow is at its peak, production has peaked for the organization in its present state.

Most ministries don't recognize the need for change until Point B, when production has begun to decline. Handy argues that leaders must have the foresight to predict trends, and change before decline sets in, at Point A. This is difficult, because no one else sees a need to "fix" what isn't broken.

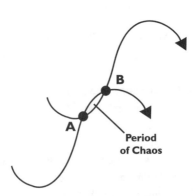

Period of Chaos...

If the leader makes the change at Point A, he will incur the misunderstanding of others. For the season between Point A and Point B—the organization will experience a period of "chaos" in which everyone feels they are in a state of "flux," routines are disturbed, and the security of the familiar is absent. This chaos can only be avoided if the leader waits until it's obvious the change is needed—however, at this point, it is too late to stay on top of the game. We must change before the decline.

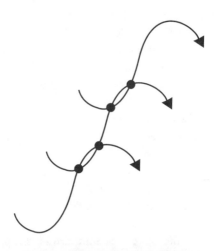

Period of Chaos

Constant Growth means Consistent Chaos!

Consequently, if an organization desires to stay on top, they are literally inviting chaos to be their constant companion, as in the diagram on the right. There will be a consistent trend of change, growth, recognition for more change—and chaos. If leaders and organizations are secure enough to endure it, this chaotic, flexible mode of operation will save their future. The fact of the matter is—all of us will change with the future. The question is: will it be too late? Eric Hoffer wrote: "In times of change, the 'learners' will inherit the earth, while the 'knowers' will find themselves beautifully equipped to deal with a world that no longer exists."

Does it Really Make Any Difference?

Let me close with some good news. God has raised up men and women in every generation who are committed to developing collegians as leaders. Consider the ministry of August Hermann Franke, who lived back in the 17th century. My friend Steve Moore once said, "Franke's influence on young leaders is a tributary to kingdom impact that flowed from his headwaters to countless others."

Franke was an effective leader with a passion for developing others. His philosophy was much like ours—be both practical and biblical. One of Franke's students at Halle University in Germany (1663-1727) was Nicholas Ludwig von Zinzendorf. Count Zinzendorf came to Halle and spent six years under Franke as a teenager. He got connected to key resources and missionaries while there as a student. In his early 20s, Zinzendorf opened his inherited property to refugees who were suffering for their faith. It was there that the Moravian movement was born and hundreds of missionaries were sent out.

Change is in the wind, and I believe the Holy Spirit is the author.

A group of Moravian missionaries, in the providence of God, were on the same ship with John Wesley as he traveled to Georgia to serve among the American Indians. During the stormy ride, Wesley was impressed with the calm and peaceful demeanor of the Moravians. He sought the counsel of Peter Bohler (another Moravian) from whom he became convinced of his own spiritual barrenness. Wesley eventually traveled to see Count Zinzendorf for counsel.

Among the tens of thousands influenced by Wesley was John Newton. Though not a Methodist himself, Newton's correspondence with Wesley shows how much he was impacted by him. Newton passed along a divine passion to clergyman named Thomas Scott, who by his own admission had no experience of the Spirit's grace until touched by the sharing of John Newton. With this newfound passion, Thomas Scott preached with vigor in his local church. A young leader in the congregation was profoundly impacted. That young leader was William Carey, who became the Father of Protestant Missions.

At a strategic moment in Carey's journey, when it seemed his fellow Baptists were going to give up on the dream of forming a missionary society, he found strength in the story of the Moravian movement and the life example of Zinzendorf—which takes us full circle to the influence of Hermann Franke and his work at Halle University with young leaders. As I reflect on this, I literally thank God that August Hermann Franke was committed to developing students! His legacy still impacts us today.

Drawing a Conclusion

What I have challenged you to do in this chapter is heavy. Some might call it radical. It certainly is a cry to do more than status quo on your campus and in your church program with collegians. I am asking you to be a change agent—to step out of any rut you might be in, and make your goal to develop ministers and leaders from collegians you know. Change is in the wind, and I believe the Holy Spirit is the author.

When all is said and done, we believe there are a handful of conclusions that can be drawn regarding the art of "student development." If a church or school is to consistently produce quality ministers and leaders from their constituents, it is optimal that the pastor or leaders embrace the following principles:

- A church or campus will see consistent streams of leaders emerge each year only as they intentionally establish systems to foster their collegiate leadership development.
- A university pastor or campus minister must see his role not merely as shepherd to the flock, but equipper of the flock.
- A structure must be created that builds a student at each "station" or phase of growth they experience in the local church or school campus.
- Collegiate leaders must make the following decisions for themselves and the staff they hire:
    a. The leader is first a "model," because while we teach what we know, we reproduce what we are. Students will follow the lead of the leader.
    b. The leader is a "minister," because while he/she does perform leadership functions beyond that of a minister, she can never leave behind the function of servanthood.
    c. The leader is a "mentor," because he/she now is selecting students and intentionally investing his or her life into them.
    d. The leader is a "monitor," because managing the system and "fishing" for potential students at each level of the structure becomes paramount. He is a recruiter.
    e. The collegiate leader is a "mobilizer," because he must keep the "heat" on for his or her students to grow and stretch and become who they need to be spiritually.

While we teach what we know, we reproduce what we are.

To which of the eight myths about leadership development do you feel the most susceptible? How can you combat that myth? In the space below, jot down your thoughts.

Think about the story you want your organization to write. What do you envision people saying about your collegiate program at your church or campus years from now?

What structures do you currently have in place to develop leadership for collegiate ministry? Based on the principles of this chapter, how can you improve them? What new structures do you need to add? If you have one or two ideas you want to remember, jot them down below.

Think It Over, Write It Down

Take a moment and jot down what you believe to be good steps of change, in light of this chapter on developing student leaders:

Further Reading

The Master Plan of Evangelism, Robert Coleman, Spire Books, 1963
The Disciple-Making Pastor, Bill Hull, Baker Books, 1999
Aqua Church, Leonard Sweet, Group Publishers
Mentoring: How to Invest Your Life in Others, Tim Elmore, EQUIP, 1995
The Bible on Leadership, Lorin Woolfe, AMACOM Publishers, 2002
The Circle of Innovation, Tom Peters, Random House, 1999

Building Champions

RECRUITING AND RELEASING
A GREAT TEAM OF VOLUNTEERS

*"Go, therefore, and make disciples of all nations, baptizing them
in the name of the Father and of the Son and of the Holy Spirit,
teaching them to observe everything I have commanded you."*
—Matthew 28:19-20 (HCSB®)

*"He who does the work is not so profitably employed
as he who multiplies the workers."—John R. Mott*

Henrietta Mears is one of my heroes of college ministry. For years during the middle part of
the 20th century she ministered to university students at Hollywood Presbyterian Church.
She was a single woman with a passion to raise up "laborers for the harvest." She was the
inspiration and genius behind the great Sunday School that mushroomed at the church.
Founder of Gospel Light Publications, she also saw her dream of a Bible conference center at
Forest Home become a reality.

Mears was quite a lady. Her passion for college students didn't end, however, with attracting
them to Sunday School. Her real passion was calling them into service. She believed every student was called not only to be a disciple of Jesus, but a worker for Jesus. She set high standards for ministry and leadership, and challenged her students to meet them. One year, none
of her students qualified for a leadership position. They failed to demonstrate the commitment and meet the standards she had set. Do you know what she did? She removed all the
names on the election ballot, and announced that no one met the standard. The ministry was
without student leaders that entire year. Mears herself discipled students so that the following
year it would be different.

One might think Mears's high standards would repel students. It was quite the opposite. Not
only did her ministry swell, but she attracted and equipped some of today's most influential
leaders. Richard Halverson was trained by Mears, and not only pastored great churches, but
became chaplain of the U.S. Senate. Have you heard of Bill Bright? Mears mentored him when
he was a student at UCLA and challenged him to begin his "campus crusade" across the
country. How about Billy Graham? He once said, "I knew Henrietta Mears for approximately
15 years. She has had a remarkable influence, both directly and indirectly, on my life. In fact, I
doubt if any other woman outside my wife and mother has had such a marked influence."[1]

Prior to assuming her leadership role at Hollywood Presbyterian Church, Mears laid out her
commitment to equipping college students:
1. I will win the personal allegiance of every student in my Sunday School class to the Lord
   and Master, by talking, writing and praying. I will expect a decision on the part of each
   one, and I will make sure that decision is based on facts. No boy or girl will I ever give
   up on as unreachable.
2. I will not think my work over when my pupil has made his decision for Christ. I will help
   him to realize how necessary daily Bible reading and prayer are. I will also put helpful
   books in his hands, and will encourage him to unite with God's people. I will show him
   the importance of church work. In all this, I will stay close until he is established, remaining at all times accessible to him.

> "I will win the
> personal allegiance
> of every student
> in my Sunday School
> class to the Lord
> and Master, by talking,
> writing, and praying."
> —Henrietta Mears

Dr. Semmelweis tried everything to figure out why so many women were dying. Some ladies were so afraid of going into his maternity ward that they actually gave birth out on the street, then went in to the hospital! Gradually, Dr. Semmelweis began to conclude there was a correlation between the research he did on cadavers in another part of their hospital and the failure he had on the maternity ward. The doctors were working on dead bodies, then running over to help women in labor five minutes later! From his observations, he developed a theory of childbed fever—that became the precursor to germ theory. Once he began requiring doctors to wash their hands in a chlorine and lime solution before treating a maternity patient, the death rate fell to one in 100. His theory was right.[2]

Semmelweis later remarked, "Only God knows the number of patients who went prematurely to their graves because of me." Wow. Can you imagine?

This true story is sad enough by the fact that so many women died needlessly from germs. What makes it doubly sad is that the people in charge were the carriers. Get the message? It was the leaders who had unwittingly created such a toxic culture.

As you perform your assessment on your ministry, either in the church or on the campus, don't step back so far that you begin to intellectualize the whole thing. Don't distance yourself so much that you miss how you are affecting the culture. Either positively or negatively—you're contagious.

To help you see things clearly, I suggest you assess your ministry from four angles:

From INSIDE the ministry
See what you're doing from the perspective
    of those you work alongside.

From a CURRENT point of view
What does your situation look like
    from where you are now?

From OUTSIDE the ministry
See what you're doing from the perspective
    of someone who does not normally attend.

From a FUTURE point of view
What will your situation look like
    years from now? Do you see trends?

Envision
Charles Darrow had a vision. His dream was to become a millionaire. This was an especially big goal in the 1920s. He even married his wife on the premise that they would be millionaires. Unfortunately, 1929 rolled around. The stock market crashed and the Great Depression began. The Darrows lost almost everything. They lost their jobs, their car, and they had to mortgage their home. Soon Charles told his wife he'd given up on the dream. She responded that they couldn't give up on the dream. It would just take some time, and they needed to stay active keeping the dream alive as they waited. Charles decided to follow her counsel. He and his wife began to sit down each night and pretend they had a million dollars. Each told the other what they would do with their half of the money. They did this for several months. The exercise soon got old, so they decided to create some play money, and actually exchange it back and forth. After a while, they began to add other elements to their game such as homes, hotels, dice, and cards…and, you guessed it. By 1932, Charles Darrow and his wife had created the first game of Monopoly—right in the middle of the Great Depression. They continued developing the pieces until 1935 when Parker Brothers bought the game from Charles Darrow. Do you know how much money they paid him for it? Right again. One million dollars!

What a picture of the power of keeping your dream alive. How much more should we, who serve the living God? We have a mission far greater than a million bucks! Our problem usually lies in one of two areas. Either we've never paused long enough to distill what our vision is, or we have given up on it as we matured, thinking we have just grown up. Let me ask you: do you know exactly what your God-given vision is for your ministry? If so, are you taking steps each week toward the fulfillment of that vision? Or have you given up?

Either positively or negatively—you're contagious.

Do you know exactly what your God-given vision is for your ministry?

3. I will see that he finds a definite place in some specified task. I will not rest until every student is an out-and-out aggressive Christian, for God has a place for each one to serve.

4. I will bring Christianity out of the unreal into the everyday life. I will show my students the practical things they should be doing as Christians. The ministrations that the world needs so much today—meat for the hungry, drink for the thirsty—are judgment-day tests of genuine Christianity (Matt. 25).

5. I will try to help each one discover the will of God, because the Master can use every talent. I will try to see in them what God sees. Michelangelo saw the face of an angel in a discarded stone. Christ saw a writer in a tax gatherer, a preacher in a fisherman, a world evangelist in a murderer. He takes the foolish things to work His purposes.

6. I will instill a divine discontent into the mind of everyone who can do more than he is doing, not by telling him the pettiness of his life, but by giving him a vision of great things to be done enthusiastically, passionately.

7. I will make it easy for anyone to come to me with the deepest experiences of his inner life, not by urging but by sympathy and understanding. I will never let anyone think I am disappointed in him.

8. I will put the cross back in the Christian life. "It is great to be out where the fight is strong, to be where the heaviest troops belong, and to fight there for God and man."

9. I will pray as I have never prayed before for wisdom and power, believing God's promise that "if any of you lack wisdom, let him ask…and it shall be given him."

10. I will spend and be spent in this battle. I will not seek rest and ease. I will not think that freshness of face holds beauty in comparison with the glory of heaven. I will seek fellowship with the Man of sorrows, acquainted with grief, as He walks through the stricken world. I will not fail Him.[2]

Question: *How well do you equip and mobilize collegiate volunteers?*

Is It In the Bible?

This idea of mobilizing workers and leaders is actually God's idea. When Moses led the people of Israel, like us, he complained about the heavy responsibility he carried. Hearing his complaints, God instructed him to do what he should have done earlier: share the load. He told Moses to identify, prepare, and release 70 other leaders to help him lead. According to Numbers 11:16-30, God was explicit in detailing what those 70 leaders would need from Moses as he equipped them:

- They need authority (v. 16, "Bring Me 70 men...have them stand there with you.")
- They need anointing (v. 17, "I will take some of the Spirit…and put the Spirit on them.")
- They need ownership of the vision (v. 17, "The Spirit who is on you…on them")
- They need responsibility (v. 17, "They will help you bear the burden.")
- They need specific ministry roles (v. 24, "Had them stand around the tent")
- They need to express their gifts (v. 25, "As the Spirit rested on them, they prophesied.")
- They need a secure shepherd who will release them to succeed (vv. 26-30: Moses)

You should see this isn't the story of a leader "dumping" work on others. Nor was it a leader merely delegating work. It is the story of a leader developing others to share ownership of the work. It is about a leader preparing others to lead. This topic is discussed in more length in the book on mentoring in this series, *Intentional Influence: Investing Your Life Through Mentoring.*

This story is also recorded in Exodus 18:19-26. Moses made some revolutionary changes in the way he led the nation, once he decided to stop doing it all and train other leaders. Notice seven changes Moses made in his leadership, as he mobilized the elders:

"I will spend and be spent in this battle."
—Henrietta Mears

Always look for character, desire, and potential.

- He became a man of prayer (v. 19).
- He committed himself to communication (v. 20).
- He laid out the vision (v. 20).
- He developed a plan (v. 20).
- He selected and trained the leaders according to their ability (v. 21).
- He released them to do the work (v. 22).
- He did only what they could not do (v. 22).

The result in Moses' ministry? God supplied strength for Moses to last for the long haul, and He gave peace to the people because their needs were met (v. 23).

If we will give a large percentage of our time to developing workers and leaders, we'll find those workers will take care of many of the tasks we used to do ourselves. It's about multiplication, not mere addition. This is what Paul had in mind when he wrote Timothy:

"And what you have heard from me in the presence of many witnesses,
commit to faithful men who will be able to teach others also" (2 Tim. 2:2).

So How Do We Do It?

Let's spend the rest of this chapter outlining the steps to building a team of collegiate champions. There is a process to recruiting and equipping volunteers to help you carry the load.

Choose Them Right
When it comes to identifying laborers and leaders, I find no biblical precedent for democratic elections. Certainly, there is nothing wrong with the local body of Christ confirming God-given leaders to guide them. However, Scripture endorses divine selection, not democratic election. Jesus selected His 12 disciples, He didn't take a vote. If you lead a ministry that uses elections and ballots, I suggest you assemble a very good nominating committee that understands biblical qualifications for ministry and leadership. Always have them look for character, desire, and potential.

When looking for disciples to develop, I always look for FAITH:
- F — Faithful
- A — Available
- I — Initiative
- T — Teachable
- H — Hungry

When looking for leaders to develop, I always look for GIFTS:
- G — Gifted with public gifts
- I — Influential with peers
- F — Fruitful in their work
- T — Trustworthy heart
- S — Serving somewhere already

I recognize these lists seem idealistic. However, I found that Henrietta Mears was right when she set a biblical standard for leadership, and stuck to it. We get into trouble the moment we compromise the standards. Keep it high. Keep searching. A reporter once asked Andrew Carnegie how he had hired 43 millionaires. Carnegie responded that those men had not been millionaires when they started working for him, but had become millionaires as a result.

The reporter's next question: "How did you develop these men to become so valuable to you that you have paid them this much money?" Carnegie replied that men are developed the

"When you mine for gold," he said, "several tons of dirt must be moved to get to an ounce of gold; but one doesn't go looking for dirt— one goes looking for gold."

If they possess a heart for the task, the rest will often follow.

same as gold is mined. "When you mine for gold," he said, "several tons of dirt must be moved to get to an ounce of gold; but one doesn't go looking for dirt—one goes looking for gold."

Don't worry if the potential worker is rough around the edges. You are not looking for a polished leader, but for a potential leader. Ability may lie deep underneath the surface and you must dig for it, just as Carnegie taught. May I remind you that many of the world's most influential people were rough and unpolished in the beginning. Some were even slow starters:

- Michael Jordan was cut from his high school basketball team his freshman year.
- Walt Disney was fired by a newspaper because they thought he had no good ideas.
- Albert Einstein couldn't speak until he was four years old, and didn't read until age seven.
- According to Beethoven's music teacher, "As a composer, [Beethoven] is hopeless."
- His teachers said young Thomas Edison was so stupid he'd never learn anything.
- Missile and satellite expert Dr. Werner Von Braun flunked math as a teenager.
- An expert said of famous football coach Vince Lombardi: "He possesses minimal football knowledge. Lacks motivation."
- Sir Isaac Newton finished next to the lowest in his class and failed geometry.
- Eighteen publishers rejected Richard Bach's story, *Jonathan Livingston Seagull*. Macmillan finally published it, and by 1975 it sold more than seven million copies in the U.S.
- After Fred Astaire's first screen test, the MGM director said: "Can't act. Slightly bald. Can dance a little." (Astaire hung that memo in his Beverly Hills home!)

People You'll Want to Find

When searching for a student to serve in a ministry, always locate one with a heart for that particular ministry. If they possess a heart for the task, the rest will often follow. Once you've found people with a heart for their task, you find students who can fill the following roles:

POSITION	DESCRIPTION	WHO DOES THIS?
1. Attractor	Magnetically attracts new people	_____
2. Idea Person	Good thinker; creatively sparks new ideas	_____
3. Implementer	Takes ideas and implements them	_____
4. People Processor	Loves to assimilate people into the group	_____
5. Critical Thinker	Sees objectively; spots potential problems	_____
6. Back-Door Closer	Maintains relationships; follows up	_____
7. Organizer	Administers and organizes details	_____
8. Visionary	Consistently calls people to the big picture	_____
9. Developer	Empowers, mentors, and develops ministers	_____

Question: *How do you select student workers? What's your criteria?*

Charge Them Up
The second step is to equip them for their ministry. God never gives someone a task without preparing them for it. Neither should we. There are two extremes we must avoid. Dr. Howard Hendricks has said for years: "Education without application is abortion." I agree. That's one

extreme we must never commit. Teach for obedience, not merely information. However, I believe it's just as bad to hand out a job, but fail to equip a student for it. When we give no resources to them, we often set them up to fail.

The term *resource* is an extraordinary word. Its root, *source,* comes from the Latin verb that connotes *rising or lifting up.* The prefix *re* means *again.* The word has come to mean *a source of supply for enabling something to be carried on.* Resources enable students to move forward and accomplish their task.[3]

It is essential that those in collegiate work begin to see ourselves as equippers—actually doing the work of equipping. We are not merely shepherds, not merely teachers, not merely activity directors. We are equippers of the saints to do the work of the ministry (Eph. 4:10-11).

It is essential that those in collegiate work begin to see ourselves as equippers—actually doing the work of equipping.

Jesus' Idea

In the book, *Intentional Influence: Investing Your Life Through Mentoring,* I discuss the Master Equipper of all time: Jesus Christ. As you read the Gospels again, I dare you to see Jesus through the lens of an equipper and mentor. He is amazing. He took those 12 emerging leaders and developed them into effective ministers and leaders. So effective were they, they reached entire nations in short periods of time (Acts 19:10).

As I study the Gospels, I notice Jesus fulfilling four functions with His students. You might say this is Jesus' IDEA for developing potential leaders:

I   Instruction in a life-related context.—*He took time to teach them verbally, explaining kingdom principles.*

D   Demonstration in a life-related context.—*He not only spoke the principles, He modeled for them as an example for His men.*

E   Experience in a life-related context.—*It wasn't just "show and tell." He allowed them to experience ministry firsthand.*

A   Assessment in a life-related context.—*Finally He evaluated their experience, assessing their hearts and their actions.*

Question: *How do you implement Jesus' IDEA of equipping laborers through your campus ministry?*

I — INSTRUCTION _____

D — DEMONSTRATION _____

E — EXPERIENCE _____

A — ASSESSMENT _____

Resources enable students to move forward and accomplish their task.

Richard was one of those collegians who felt he'd never be a leader. I remember when he first attended our group years ago. He was introverted, quiet, and hesitant to sign up for any activity beyond our Sunday morning class. If he had any goal, it was to simply warm a seat on Sunday. Because I saw potential in him he obviously did not see, it was work to get him involved. It took an entire semester to get him into a small group. Once he felt he was part of a community, I decided to take the next step. I asked him to serve on our media team. It took another semester for him to say yes. The following year, I challenged him to be discipled. I found the perfect mentor for him, someone who also was a bit shy by nature, but mature. Once they began, things began to change more rapidly. Soon he believed he could make a difference. During his third year, he served on our collegian council. By his final year in our group, Richard led a small group, led the media team, and discipled two other men.

"I am forever grateful, and will spend my life discipling other men because of the model I saw during my years in college."

What I love most about Richard's story is that years later he took the time to express himself to me. He wrote: "I am a different person now than when I first came to the collegian class. I was convinced I could never do anything 'spiritual' or even dream of making a difference in someone else's life. It was a big deal for me to simply show up to class. That's why I believe in the power of equipping. I had never heard the word before I came to Skyline Church. You all gave me the tools to become the man I had inside of me. I am forever grateful, and will spend my life discipling other men because of the model I saw during my years in college."

Question: *Do you equip students before giving them jobs to do? How are you "building champions?"*

Challenge Them Well

I believe most university ministers on church staff and campus ministers fail to sufficiently challenge students. We are either afraid of turning them off, or we're afraid they will simply leave our ministry. So we water down the challenge of Christ, and dance around issues such as commitment and self-denial. At best, we drop hints, hoping they'll catch them, and one day mature and be ready for adult life.

Jesus constantly challenged people, and became more attractive to them by doing so. He was a magnet. Why? I believe it's because people have potential for greatness inside of them that they'd never reach unless a leader challenges them to tap into it. Most people feel ordinary; but just as true, they want to be part of something bigger than they are. Someone once said, "There are no great men, only great challenges that ordinary men feel called to meet."

It has been said that people are like rubber bands. Until a person is stretched, it is impossible to assess his or her potential. Further, like rubber bands, I believe people are not fully useful until they are stretched. While I do not know your sharpest students personally, I can guess one quality about them. Students with high potential want a challenge that is very important and almost impossible. Big challenges attract big thinkers. In the final chapter, I will describe some examples of how you might create challenges that will develop students. For now, I suggest that a successful challenge for college students is:

- Personal
- Attainable
- Measurable
- Visible
- Expandable
- Valuable

> People are like rubber bands. Until a person is stretched, it is impossible to assess his or her potential.

Issuing the Challenge

When you locate students you want to challenge to be involved in the ministry, I suggest you consider the following sequence as you ask them to step out and do it:

1. Meet with them and get acquainted with their goals. Be sure they want to head in the same direction as you.
2. Take time to share your vision with them. Don't detail the tasks before you give them a clear, big-picture perspective of your dream. Share your passion.
3. Ask where they believe they might fit into the vision you've described. Let them respond and participate in discussing the big idea with you.
4. Allow them to think and pray about it. Don't pressure them for an immediate answer.
5. Schedule a time to meet again and discuss questions and next steps.

As a collegiate leader, I need to remember that I cannot authentically challenge my students unless I am living a challenged life myself. Students don't follow mediocrity with passion. Students don't pay for average. I have some questions I ask myself before I challenge students:

- Do students become passionate about Jesus and His kingdom when around me?
- Do I make others feel good about themselves and their potential?
- Do I add value to others whenever I contact them?
- Do students easily receive truth from me?
- Do I model the values I want my students to embrace?

Students don't follow mediocrity with passion. Students don't pay for average.

When I first became a college pastor, I saw the value of challenging students and began to see this principle at work. I wanted a college group who wasn't satisfied with simply meeting together once a week. I desired a radical group who was determined to reach outsiders for Christ. So I began going out with collegians every Friday night, sharing Christ with people on the streets. Soon we had over 60 students out there following the model.

After a year, I began to share Christ with those who were attending rock concerts. When some band would come to town for a concert, we found loads of people there who were willing to talk about spiritual things. Soon I had dozens of collegians out with me at the concerts. Finally I found doors beginning to open for me to share with the musicians, celebrities, or athletes who were in town. I would find them either backstage or at a hotel afterward, and God would provide wonderful opportunities to share Christ. I had the privilege to witness to KISS, the Beach Boys, Elton John, Styx, John Denver, Olivia Newton John, John Ford Coley, and a number of athletes in the NBA, NFL, and major league baseball. It was a challenge! And can you guess who followed suit? Students. Soon I found a number of students who were finding their way into places to share the Lord with people of influence. People are simply a reflection of their leader. For better or worse, leaders attract who they are, not who they want.

Question: *Do you stretch your students spiritually with their leadership? Do you furnish new challenges in the application of their leadership so they'll reach their potential?*

Cheer Them Up
If I am going to recruit and release a team of volunteers, I must master the art of encouragement. George Adams once said, "Encouragement is the oxygen of the soul." I don't know too many collegiate leaders who have built teams of volunteers without the ability to encourage them. In fact, I believe challenge and encouragement are like two oars on a boat. You must have both of them to move forward.

Why is encouragement and affirmation so important to young leaders and workers? First, they are undergoing much change as they assume new roles. They're in unfamiliar territory. Second, they will make mistakes and feel like failures. Third, encouragement actually helps them reach their potential. An experiment was once conducted to measure people's capacity to endure pain. How long could a barefooted person stand in a bucket of ice water? It was discovered that when someone else offered encouragement and support, the person standing in the ice water could tolerate pain twice as long as when there was no one present.

Here's the rule of thumb I began practicing years ago with my volunteers. I urge you to develop your own rule of thumb with your volunteers in collegiate ministry.
- Look for good to reward in each collegiate leader.
- Affirm the college student or adult worker immediately.
- Choose not only an action but a quality to affirm in each student and worker.
- Make your affirmation both personal to them, and public before others.
- Put it in writing as often as you can.

"Encouragement is the oxygen of the soul."
—George Adams

Sister Helen Mrosla taught in a Catholic school for years. She often spoke of a difficult year when her students defied her every day. A young teen name Mark was the worst. Once, she said she even taped Mark's mouth shut for talking too much in class.

The class had worked hard all week one week, and on Friday they were getting cranky. So she thought she'd reward them. At a break, she asked them to write down the nicest thing they could about every student in the class and hand it in. She compiled the results and gave out the lists. Even Mark got one.

Several years later, Mark was killed in Vietnam. After the funeral, most of his former classmates gathered with Mark's parents and Sister Helen for lunch. Mark's father took a wallet out of his pocket. "They found this on Mark when he was killed," he said. He carefully removed a folded, refolded, and taped paper—the one on which Sister Helen listed the good things Mark's classmates had said about him. This didn't surprise anyone except Sister Helen.

Charlie smiled sheepishly and said, "I keep my list in my desk drawer."

Chuck's wife said, "Chuck put his in our wedding album."

"I have mine, too," Marilyn said, "in my diary."

Vicky reached into her pocketbook and brought out her frayed list.

People thrive on encouragement. Most never receive enough. I believe some of the stupid things students do is a result of the need for attention and affirmation. Sometimes any attention (even bad) is better than no attention. Sin is often people meeting real needs in unhealthy ways. Without encouragement, we'll never become the people we were designed to be.

Case in point. Heartbroken, Nathaniel went home to tell his wife he had been fired from his job. Sophia shocked him with an exclamation of joy. "Now you can write your book!"

"Yes," he replied with sagging confidence, "and what shall we live on while I am writing it?"

To his amazement, she opened a drawer and pulled out a substantial amount of money. "Where on earth did you get that?" he exclaimed.

"I have always known you were a man of genius," she told him. "I knew that someday you would write a masterpiece. So every week, out of the money you give me for housekeeping, I save a little bit. Here is enough to last us for one whole year."

From her confidence came one of the greatest novels of American literature, *The Scarlet Letter* by Nathaniel Hawthorne.[4]

Personal Evaluation: List the people on your team of volunteers and their value:

NAME: VALUE YOU COULD AFFIRM:

_____   _____

_____   _____

_____   _____

_____   _____

_____   _____

Question: *How frequently do you identify good qualities in others around you in your campus program and affirm them?*

> Make your affirmation both personal to them and public to others.

> Without encouragement, we'll never become the people we were designed to be.

Check Them Out

As you work with volunteers in your campus program, remember to balance expectation with inspection. Volunteers do what their leaders expect and inspect. This means we must give time to look them over and insure we've placed them in the most fruitful spot possible, for both them and the ministry as a whole. Here's a checklist for new volunteers:

- Are they doing what is expected?
- Are they learning while they are doing?
- Are they effective with other students?
- Are they ready for new challenges?

My good friend, Alan Nelson, pastors a church in Scottsdale, Arizona. Recently, he wrote a book entitled *Spirituality and Leadership*. In it, he talks about sizing up volunteer workers and leaders, and suggests a list on how to check them out or evaluate them. Take a moment and picture one of your campus volunteers. Then check them against this list.

IQ (Intelligence Quotient)

Spiritual leaders sometimes underestimate the role of IQ. This is pretty much a God-given factor. It does not reflect education, but rather a capacity to process information. Put low-IQ people in demanding situations and you'll overwhelm them, stressing them out and frustrating others. Place people with higher IQs in simple roles and you'll bore them to death.

AQ (Attitude Quotient)

Attitude is contagious, so be sure you place high-AQ people in places where they can infect other with their positive energy. Low-AQ people are negative, pessimistic, and melancholy in nature, so try to keep them in a position where their attitudes won't adversely affect other people and decision-making.

RQ (Resource Quotient)

First analyze the type of resources a person has: time, talents, and treasure (students and adult sponsors). Especially in volunteer organizations, time and treasure factors become as big as talent issues. Those who have talents but limited time must be used strategically. People with treasures but little time can provide needed capital to fund projects.

PQ (People Quotient)

High-PQ people are good relationally. They shine among others. Place these people in front-end service roles. They'll make your ministry look better than it is! Low-PQ people are good behind the scenes, where they won't bore, offend, or alienate others. Use their other gifts, but keep them out of public or team-building venues.

MQ (Maturity Quotient)

This is important to assess, especially with students. Emotional and spiritual maturity provide great stability within people. Decision-makers, mentors, and influencers need a certain level of consistency, insight, and discernment. Talented students lacking maturity are attractive but they can be organizational kindling, starting unnecessary fires.

EQ (Energy Quotient)

There are turtles and there are rabbits. You can't do a lot about energy levels. Don't overwhelm turtles or you'll lose them. Conversely, let the rabbits run, but put measures in place to ensure accuracy and completeness. Provide plenty of things to do and don't team them up with turtles that will frustrate them. High-EQs can handle a lot on their plates.

CQ (Commitment Quotient)

CQ is the key to unlock the other quotients. The greatest frustration for any leader is to have people with high quotients who lack motivation and commitment. Low-CQ people will hold back, while high-CQ people will go the extra mile. One of the primary tasks of spiritual leaders is to raise the level of commitment in followers and potential leaders.

Once you've assessed a student's quotients, the final task is matching them with a role or adjusting their role. The better you are at matching strengths with your ministry needs, the more effective you'll be.[5] Take a moment to evaluate your present collegiate workers and see how they check out against the list.

> Talented students lacking maturity are attractive, but they can be organizational kindling, starting unnecessary fires.

Volunteer	High Quotients	Low Quotients
_____	_____	_____
_____	_____	_____
_____	_____	_____
_____	_____	_____
_____	_____	_____

Question: *Do you regularly evaluate your ministry's progress?*
❑ *Yes*   ❑ *Sometime*   ❑ *Not often*   ❑ *Never*   ❑ *Would like to*

Do you assess workers?
❑ *Yes*   ❑ *Sometime*   ❑ *Not often*   ❑ *Never*   ❑ *Would like to*

Change Them Often

This final step may sound strange, but I believe we have to practice it. If we are to reproduce other leaders, we must furnish new leaders a chance to spread their wings and fly. Potential leaders need an opportunity to serve. No doubt, it is easy to leave the old ones in place. After all, they have finally learned the job they are doing. Why not enjoy a moment of rest and let them do it? The answer is simple, but it isn't easy. Because your job is to continue equipping new laborers and leaders. D. L. Moody once said, "It is better to train a hundred men than to do the work of a hundred men. But it is harder."

Years ago the president of Bell Telephone said: "Our company has a policy at every level of management. No person can stay at the same job for over five years." We had a two-year rule in our college group. Why is this so important for your ministry? First, it forces you (the leader) to develop new leaders. Next, it gives the experienced leaders a new challenge. Third, it gives the opportunity for potential leaders to serve. Finally, it enhances creativity by putting new blood into the workforce. New ideas most often come from new people who see things from a different perspective. They aren't stuck in a rut.

This doesn't mean you chuck the older leaders. They are far too experienced. It means you must find or create new places for them to use their experience. As a college pastor, I created higher level positions for senior volunteers and interns. They actually oversaw most of the leaders in our ministry "funnel." In fact, I ultimately gave my time to level 1 and level 5 activities on that funnel. I spoke at our weekly rally and I trained the leaders of leaders. Everything else was led by experienced student leaders. But only after they were equipped to do so.

Raising the Bar

I recognize I am challenging you with a huge task. You might even be thinking this is impossible; that you don't have enough workers to follow my suggestions; that I don't really understand college students today. Those are natural feelings, when the bar has been raised so high that it's difficult to reach. I have felt that way, too, when I've been challenged by others. Let me assure you of one thing, however. This is possible. The college ministries throughout history that have had lasting impact have been ones that determined they were going to set high standards and equip students to serve and to lead.

Even on tough campuses like yours—God has managed to transform the spiritual culture. For instance, many view students of the 18th or 19th century as basically fine, upstanding citizens with morals and manners. After all, the early colleges were primarily church-related. Didn't they have godly instructors and saintly students? Well, that depends on the school, the time, and the student leaders. Visit, for example, Yale College at the turn of the 18th century. The impact of the French revolution upon western society had led to the corruption of both culture and mind. Lyman Beecher, a student at Yale during that time, described Yale in this way:

"Before our new president came, the college was in a most ungodly state. The college church was almost extinct. Most of the students were skeptical, and rowdies were plenty. Wine and liquor were kept in many rooms; intemperance, profanity, gambling, and licentiousness were common."[6]

Hmmm. Sound familiar? And Yale wasn't alone. Princeton had its share of rowdies. In 1780, half the student body participated in a "serious riot" to protest a decision by the administration to suspend several pupils for an offense most considered minor. Guns were fired, dorm walls and doors defaced, and general chaos prevailed. Only when the president threatened to shut down the place until the trustees met did disorder cease.[7]

Harvard was also plagued with what S. E. Morrison called "French Mania." He said the typical student was an atheist, an experimentalist in morals, and a rebel to authority. You may be surprised to know that similar reports were given at Williams College, Brown University, Hampden-Sydney College, and Bowdoin College.

What's my point? Simply that collegiate ministry has always been a challenge. At the same time, there have been campus ministers, faculty, staff, or university pastors who somehow reached them, cast vision to them, and equipped them to be revolutionaries for Christ. Those same schools I listed above experienced major movements of God's Spirit, and at one point revival broke out on campus. At Yale in 1802, a spiritual revival occurred that "shook the institution to its center."[8] Each of these schools have stories of how God broke through to students—usually through students.

Today it is tough to impact a college student for Jesus. I know that. Nevertheless, that's why God called you there. You are there to grow those students into revolutionaries. Your job is building champions. You are a leader!

Question: *Are you ready to raise the bar at your campus? Are you ready to take risks on new leaders from among your presently involved students?*

> The college ministries throughout history that have had lasting impact have been ones that determined they were going to set high standards and equip students to serve and to lead.

Assessment

1. Evaluate yourself on the six stages of developing student volunteers:

Choose Them Right	1	2	3	4	5	6	7	8	9	10
Charge Them Up	1	2	3	4	5	6	7	8	9	10
Challenge Them Well	1	2	3	4	5	6	7	8	9	10
Cheer Them Up	1	2	3	4	5	6	7	8	9	10
Check Them Out	1	2	3	4	5	6	7	8	9	10
Change Them Often	1	2	3	4	5	6	7	8	9	10

2. What steps could you take to improve where you are weak as a leader developing volunteers?

3. List some students you should challenge to serve through spiritual leadership on campus.

We must
develop people
as we delegate work.

Further Reading

Leadership Is an Art, Max Depree, Dell Publishers, 1989
The 21 Irrefutable Laws of Leadership, John Maxwell, Thomas Nelson, 1998
The 17 Indisputable Laws of Teamwork, John Maxwell, Thomas Nelson, 2001
The Making of a Leader, J. Robert Clinton, Navpress, 1988
Wired For Influence, Tim Elmore, Lifeway Christian Resources, 2002

Leaders Everywhere!

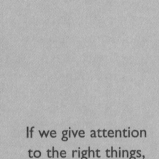

CREATING A LEADERSHIP CULTURE

"And what you have heard from me in the presence of many witnesses, commit to faithful men who will be able to teach others also.
—2 Timothy 2:2 (HCSB®)

"We are about movements, not programs. Programs usually start big, then fizzle. Movements usually start very small, then grow very large."

In 1990, the crime rate peaked in New York City. All through the 1980s violent crimes such as murder, rape, and drug traffic rose until 1990. Then the rate began to plummet. Within five years, murders were down by 64.3%. Drug traffic was cut in half in some of the worst parts of town. Other serious crimes were down almost 75%[1] A new culture had been created.

From my reading, it seems a handful of people were responsible. George Kelling had begun to work what he called the "broken-windows theory." He determined that criminals were committing crimes in areas where there were always broken windows. The broken windows signaled everyone that no one was watching over that area, that no one cared. Instead of spending money on more police officers, he figured he'd fix the broken windows, and see what happened. It worked. Repairing the windows had provided a new environment. The drug dealers, rapists, and murderers virtually left. David Gunn used the theory on New York's street gangs. He cleaned up the graffiti and kept it clean. Gang activity dropped. William Bratton used the theory on the subway system. He zeroed in on fare-beaters, people who refused to pay the subway fare to ride. This little move proved to be exactly what was necessary to change the atmosphere there. Violent crimes went way down, due to his stationing guards at the turnstiles to make sure everyone paid for their ride. All three of these men verified one thing. If we give attention to the right things, small changes can make a big difference.

What if we were to apply this truth to our campus ministries? Can relatively small changes in the church or campus make a difference in the culture on our campus? in the dorms? in our ministries? in our communities? in our nation? Charles Simeon would say absolutely yes.

Charles was an Anglican minister who served during the 19th century. Those in his parish felt he was far too radical, so they often refused to let him in the pulpit! He desperately wanted to change the "lukewarm" Church of England. So he decided to make a change in his ministry. He took a parish next to Cambridge University so he could spend time with students. He spoke in chapel as often as he was allowed. Following his messages, he would invite students to a weekly gathering he called a "conversation group." During these meetings, he would go deeper with the students since they attended voluntarily. They wanted to be there. From this group, he would hand-pick sharp student leaders who planned to enter the ministry and invite them to his home each week for a "supper club." There he would disciple and train them in a small mentoring group, preparing them for leadership in the church. Finally he chose to spend extra time with some final-year students who were almost ready to take a parish in the Church of England. This was his inner circle. He passed on the passion and principles they needed.[2]

At the time, the Anglican Church had a system that allowed the wealthy to control what preacher would fill their pulpit. Those who gave the most money could choose a nice, safe

> If we give attention to the right things, small changes can make a big difference.

minister to preach to them—one who wouldn't rock the boat. Charles Simeon decided he would raise funds so he could donate what was needed to place his passionate, young disciples in those pulpits! Working within the system, this man was used by God to transform the Church at that time. When Charles Simeon died, one-third of the pulpits in the Anglican Church were filled with his trained, young leaders!

Charles Simeon made little changes that changed the culture in England. William Bratton made some little changes that changed the culture in New York City. My question for you is: *what changes are you willing to make to transform the culture on your campus?*

I constantly hear this complaint from those who work with students: I just wish we had more leaders around here! It seems we're always looking for sharp leaders, yet never seem to create a culture that produces them. What campus program wouldn't want a "leadership culture" to emerge in their midst, where leaders naturally grow and develop within the student body? But what do we mean by the word *culture*? Let's start by defining terms.

> Culture (n): *An environment where people possess shared values, behaviors, and qualities that set them apart from others.*

Every college ministry has an organizational culture, good or bad. Most colleges or ministries don't enjoy a leadership culture. They suffer from a chronic lack of quality leaders. Staff members often have little training in leadership. They hope that student leaders will transfer from other schools, or that they'll learn leadership simply from the challenges of student life. Unfortunately, it usually doesn't happen that way. A leadership culture emerges when someone champions the cause of leadership and works a plan to create that environment. This is true of almost every movement in history.

What We Learn from History

Cultures arise out of movements not programs. Programs usually start big, then fizzle. Movements usually start small, then get very big. It's like a mustard seed. If you study how movements began in history, you find there is a pattern:

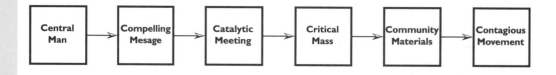

| Central Man | → | Compelling Mesage | → | Catalytic Meeting | → | Critical Mass | → | Community Materials | → | Contagious Movement |

I have already mentioned John Wesley in previous chapters. He was a man who God used to transform England during the 18th century. He didn't try to start a movement. Yet, that's what happened under his leadership. You can see from his example above that his message was taken by horseback to cities across England. He held "circuit meetings" where he would preach. His converts were organized into small groups called "class meetings" and given questions and materials to review. He was so methodical, the people called him the Great Methodist. He founded the Methodist denomination.

Leadership culture emerges when someone champions the cause of leadership and works a plan to create that environment

Cultures arise out of movements, not programs.

Here's what's amazing. Historians tell us that only 1-2% of the British population was even on board with his movement. In other words, he did so much with a relatively small amount of people. Little changes can make a big difference.

If you're reading closely, you may have noticed that movements surface through both catalytic events and a consistent process that follows. One ignites. The other insures follow through. I've found that students grow into leaders through both "events" and "process." We need events to work as a catalyst for growth. But we need process to instill the changes over time. The events are fun. The process is usually very unglamorous. In our ministry, we've placed far too much emphasis on events and far too little emphasis on process. Both are necessary, but we frequently neglect the power of process:

Event	Process
Encourages decisions	Encourages development
Motivates people	Matures people
Is a calendar issue	Is a consistency issue
Usually is about a big group	Usually is about a small group
Challenges people	Changes people
Becomes a catalyst	Becomes a culture
Is easy	Is difficult

The Event versus the Process

George Whitfield was a contemporary of John Wesley. George was actually a better orator than Wesley, and introduced Wesley to field preaching. However, George never had a movement follow him. Why not? He never organized the process after his events like Wesley did. Great meetings. Little process. Sound familiar? Whitfield himself admitted that his legacy was a "rope of sand."

Question: *Do you experience fruitful events? Do you experience a fruitful process?*

How We Develop Values

If our first conclusion is that a culture emerges through both events and process, our second conclusion must deal with how values are transferred to students. Have you ever wondered who is most influential in your students' lives? Why do students embrace certain values that seem so different from their mom and dad back home? Values are being transferred all the time—negative and positive. We need to figure out how to get in on the game.

Students develop values differently, depending on their age. Dr. Rick and Kathy Hicks have written about this in their book, *Boomers, Xers and Other Strangers*. In different periods of a young person's life, value development has different areas of focus:

Age 1-7	Age 8-13	Age 14-20	Age 21-up
Imprint by Observation	Modeling by Heroes	Socialization by Peers	Significant Emotional Event
(Patterning)	(Identification)	(Key Relationship)	(A Challenge to Change)

Students grow through both *events* and *process*.

Key events cause them to evaluate their values or enhance them.

While in college, there is a vital blend of key ingredients: relationships and significant events.

In their earliest years, students acquire values almost exclusively at home. During ages 1-7, they're communicated through "imprint by observation." Whatever Mom does is right. Children are too young to distinguish between an acceptable and an unacceptable value.

During ages 8-13, values are picked up from the model their heroes give them. They are now old enough to choose their heroes. They tend to willfully emulate them, whether they are athletes, TV stars, friends, relatives, or parents.

By their teenage years, the method of value transfer is socialization by peers. At this point, the student begins to test their values against their friend's values, to see what works for them. Key peer relationships now play a vital role in values and behavior.

Finally, at about 20 years of age, the student moves to an adult method of acquiring values. That method is significant emotional events. They are old enough for events to spark a change they want to make, even though they need follow up to make it permanent. Key events cause them to evaluate their values or enhance them.

You will notice that during the years you minister to them, students embrace values through two primary ways. While in college, there is a vital blend of key ingredients: relationships and significant events that challenge them. Consequently, we can see the crucial role of both "events" and "process" in their growth. A leadership culture will depend on the creation and wise use of both of the following:
• Significant events
• Safe environments

For example, an Atlanta-area church experiences three environments. Each one encourages the person to grow beyond events and participate in a new level of relationships:

• Foyer Environment (Sunday morning worship: goal is challenge and get acquainted)
• Living-Room Environment (Area fellowships: goal is equipping within an affinity group)
• Kitchen Environment (Community groups: goal is intimate relationship and life change)

They have recognized that growth and change happen best in the midst of a safe community and among developmental relationships. Using our terms here, they are using both events and process to foster life change. Thousands have embraced kingdom values because of the church's effective use of these environments. By the time a person reaches the kitchen environment, they are up close with a model of healthy spiritual leadership.

Question: *What kind of environments have you created that foster life change and leadership in your church or campus collegiate program? Would this be healthy for students in your program?*

Six Conclusions

After carefully examining the conclusions drawn in a report sponsored by the Kellogg Foundation,[3] and after interacting with nearly 100,000 college students, I have drawn the following conclusions about leadership development among collegians:

1. Leaders are made, not born.
Although some personalities are prone to take charge more than others, leadership is a learned art. This doesn't mean all of them will become the next Colin Powell or Mother Teresa. It means that leadership qualities and skills can and must be learned. On a scale of 1 to 10, a student may never be a 10. They may only demonstrate the leadership ability of a 4. However, by studying leadership, they could move from a 4 to a 6 or 7 on that scale. Just as disciples are made not born, so it is with leaders.

2. Students require a catalyst to begin the journey.

While some students are more natural leaders than others, all must take the journey toward maturity. Most students need a catalyst to see how God could use their influence in a significant way. This catalyst is the "event" we discussed earlier, where you introduce to students that they could lead at some level; they're called to be salt and light.

3. Becoming a leader is a process not an event.

To review, students do not turn into disciples or leaders overnight. Even if they choose to become leaders at an event, they will need the day-in, day-out support and accountability to internalize it all. I suggest you never plan an event without planning a process that follows it, helping students apply the truth they have learned.

4. Students learn leadership best in communities.

While some may debate this, I don't think we can thoroughly teach leadership over the Internet or through reading a book alone. Leadership implies relationship. Most learn leadership best in a small community, where they experience a microcosm of the body of Christ—and can learn relational skills, how to give direction, how to ask questions, resolve conflict, plan events, and how to facilitate growth in others.

5. Students need a guide to help them process their experience.

While experience may be the best teacher, it doesn't always teach the truth. I've seen students have a bad experience with leadership—and draw the wrong conclusions about it. I believe students need a guide to help them process their experience, to learn the principles, and draw the right conclusions regardless of how poor their experience was.

6. In today's world, every student will need leadership skills.

Finally, I don't believe leadership is the property of a few, select, privileged people. Today's complex world demands that everyone learn leadership skills, vision, courage, relationships, planning, and more. Harland Cleveland once surveyed executives in the U.S. to see how many true opinion leaders existed. In 1955 he estimated there were about 555,000. By 1971, the number had grown to a million. By 1985, it was at least one in every 200 Americans. Today he says he's lost count, as so many leaders exist at so many different levels of an organization.[4] Influence is everywhere. The most introverted people will influence 10,000 others in an average lifetime. We must teach our students leadership. A prominent leader in the Protestant movement says that he learned more about leadership while in college in the Baptist Campus Ministry program than he had learned in a lifetime. This is a sound endorsement that leadership training is important.

How do we use these conclusions? One group has created "The Leadership Academy" where students experience eight building blocks that develop leadership values and skills. All of this takes place two weeks prior to an internship where student leaders put into practice what they have discovered in the academy.[5] Several Baptist campus programs have developed leadership training that has sent out hundreds of new leaders to campuses throughout the world because of the skills they learned while in college. Another group created "High Point: An Adventure in Servant Leadership" in which students undergo leadership training "on the field" with all types of people by working and serving at conference centers each year.

A Culture that Develops Leaders

I love baseball—I have ever since I was a kid. I especially enjoyed the World Series in 2002. The Anaheim Angels beat the San Francisco Giants in a nail-biter that lasted seven games. What made it fun for most of us is that the Angels were a bunch of nobodies—free agents who no other team claimed, or minor leaguers the team brought up. Pitcher Ben Weber described them as "a bunch of vagabonds, guys off the scrap pile and dirt bags."[6]

Leadership implies relationship.

The most introverted people will influence 10,000 others in a lifetime.

So what made the difference and caused them to be champions? The culture. The Angels' rally did not begin in October. It began in spring training. After a 2001 season in which the Angels finished 41 games out of first place and scored fewer runs than almost every other A.L. team, manager Mike Scioscia emphasized playing for the team; the importance of situational hitting and making contact. In April, unhappy with the hitter's progress, they instituted a fine system in which, for instance, players would have to cough up $100 if they didn't advance a runner from second base with no outs. Also, for two months of the season the coaching staff posted in the clubhouse a running tally of how each player fared in key situations, such as getting runners home from third base with fewer than two outs.

"We stopped posting that list because it was apparent that guys bought into the concept," bench coach Joe Madden says. "We didn't need it anymore. It became cool to put the ball in play and advance runners. It became part of the culture."[7]

It's amazing what culture does to behavior.

What can be done to create a leadership culture? Is there a comprehensive plan we can put together that fosters leadership development using process and events, safe environments and relationships, and interaction and experience?

Let me suggest a process to build leaders in your ministry. This is sort of an "accelerated leader development" plan to use each year with staff and students. In addition to strong support from your top administration, you should include the following basic ingredients:

What are the core qualities you want to foster in students?

Criteria

I suggest you first decide what you believe a leader should look like. What are the core qualities you want to foster in students? The CrossSeekers program developed by National Collegiate Ministry at LifeWay Christian Resources that has been mentioned in this series seeks to do this. Create a screen for selecting candidates with good leadership potential. While you may invite all students to an event, you should strongly encourage those who are most ready. Remember, Jesus selected His disciples. As I mentioned in the last chapter, I use the following criteria:

When I select a disciple, I look for FAITH. When I select a leader, I look for GIFTS:

F –	Faithful		G –	Gifted with public gifts
A –	Available		I –	Influential with their peers
I –	Initiative		F –	Fruitful in their present activities
T –	Teachable		T –	Trustworthy in their character
H –	Hungry		S –	Serving already in ministry

Question: *Have you developed your criteria for a leader on the campus? If not, let me encourage you to make this a priority for your ministry.*

Catalyst

Plan an event that will sufficiently cast a vision for servant leadership. It may be a single evening or a weekend event. It must be compelling, biblical, and simple. Be sure to include a vehicle for students to respond at the end regarding their interests in leadership. Some Christian campuses have begun to implement a "Leadership Emphasis Week" just like they have a Spiritual Emphasis Week. This allows you to cast seed for the call to lead and influence the world, as salt and light. It allows you to put the cookies on the bottom shelf and make leadership accessible to everyone.

Question: *When will you plan to host a catalytic event sponsored for your collegiate audience?*

Communities—Afterglow

Place the students who respond to the catalytic event into mentoring communities of 3-6 people. These small groups will meet regularly for a set time (one semester or one year). The communities will become the "labs" to discuss and practice leadership. For many of them, this will begin the process of becoming a leader.

For instance, let's say 100 students show up at your catalytic event on leadership. At the close of the event, you invite those interested to sign up to be part of a mentoring community on the subject of leadership. Suppose 50 of them sign up. You could place them in 10 groups of 5, and start them on a process of personal growth. What would you use for curriculum or materials to guide those leading the groups. This series would be excellent when your leaders are trained in how to use it wisely.

Question: *How are you using small communities to build leaders in your collegiate program?*

Challenge

Present to each of these leadership communities a challenge or problem they must solve. Come up with a significant ministry or campus challenge that they can address as a team. You might choose a group of challenges or issues that form the context of your process. (i.e. people to be moved, problems to be solved, service projects to be completed). It's optimal if they are real, not hypothetical. These problems will become the "glue" that will cause students to stick together, and the "enemy" that will cause them to work together.

Daniel Goleman has noted a number of times in the *Harvard Business Review* that these kinds of obstacles are wonderful leadership enhancers. People have it within them to solve problems, overcome obstacles, and even lead others—but they must be in a safe place to try out their wings.

Question: *What challenges can you present to these emerging collegiate leaders to solve in your own community?*

Coaches

These are the people who will assist and facilitate the learning. At first, these could be staff or adult sponsors, but later you might use students, who've experienced the process. Your coaches are the key to the experience—and will grow in their own leadership skills along the way. The coaches don't have to be experts in leadership. They are simply guides in the self-discovery process. They are a few paces ahead of the students and help the young leaders feel safe. As we will note in a moment, they may use a resource to help them guide the group, but they are the drivers to make sure students learn and participate.

Question: *Who can serve as your coaches in this process? Think of three or four students/adult volunteers.*

Consultants

Along the way, allow students to have exposure to internal and external experts in a variety of subject matters. These are quality leaders on campus or in the community who aren't required to give lots of time, but can offer wise counsel as needed for the emerging leaders. They may be business leaders, pastors, campus counselors, faculty members, or administrative staff who simply give an afternoon or evening to investing in the student groups. If they feel comfortable, they may even give their e-mail address to the students for questions that come up later. The consultants may be chosen, based on the types of challenges you've given the groups. They will provide some key advice as the students work through their problem.

Question: *Who on your campus or in your church can serve as your special leadership consultants?*

> The communities will become the "labs" to discuss and practice leadership. For many of them, this will begin the process of becoming a leader.

Curriculum

Provide a tool or resource that enables students to discuss and draw good conclusions about leadership along the way. Often a bad experience can lead to a bad conclusion, and a failure to see a principle at work. This resource should equip and foster interaction. Ideally, it should be an interactive guide, which forms discussion points during the first part of the group meetings. Once they've discussed a leadership principle, they can apply it to the challenge they are working on in the group.

"Growing Leaders" and Student Ministry Publishing at Lifeway Church Resources have partnered to create such resources for college students. You may want to check out these titles on our Web sites:

- *Authentic Influence: Leading Without Titles*
- *Wired For Influence: Skills to Lead Others*
- *Intentional Influence: Investing Your Life Through Mentoring*

Question: *What resources will you use to ensure your collegians are learning the process of spiritual leadership?*

Champion

This person orchestrates the leader development process. If you are to create a leadership culture, someone must be the "champion" to wave the flag and cast the vision. Students may get it started, but eventually the champion must be a staff person or committed volunteer if the culture is to remain. Remember: God almost always chooses and uses one person to begin a movement. God doesn't despise small beginnings. The culture begins with one.

On every campus I know that's created a leadership culture, there is a champion who sees it as their responsibility to carry the leadership banner. Sometimes it is a faculty member, sometimes it's a student or a community member, sometimes a university minister in a church, and often—it's a campus minister.

Question: *In the fall of year when your program begins anew with incoming students, who will this person be?*

It All Starts Small

You have probably heard of the ministry The Navigators. They specialize in discipleship and leadership development. Do you know that their story illustrates these principles? I tell the story in *Intentional Influence: Investing Your Life Through Mentoring.* In 1938, Dawson Trotman had begun to work with sailors on Navy ships. One day a sailor named Les Spenser approached "Daws," and asked him to help him grow as a Christian. Trotman clarified that what Les was asking for was a discipleship or mentoring relationship. It would be intense. When the young serviceman agreed, they began to meet weekly for several months. It so transformed his life that Les Spenser brought his buddy to Dawson for the same help. Trotman refused. He challenged Les to mentor his friend himself. When the two of them began to meet, Dawson began meeting with another man, making two sets of two. When they had experienced life change— all four multiplied. Then the four became eight. The eight became 16. The 16 became 32, the 32 became 64, and so on.

Those men were shipped off to other ships until at the height of World War II. These men were on 1000 ships and naval bases around the world. Soon the FBI heard about these groups and began to investigate. Commanding officers thought a cult had begun. It took those agents three solid months to interview the men because the web of disciples had become so thick. After months, they finally found the culprit who started the whole thing—Dawson Trotman. The Navigators are still around today.

Can this happen today? I think so. When I was college pastor at San Diego's Skyline Church, we began to feel the burden of reaching the city's 100,000 university students. We knew the only way we could hope to make an impact was if we had a leadership culture, filled with students who were disciples and disciple makers. So we began with a handful. I took a group of seven guys in 1983 and began to train them. Each of them multiplied. Key leaders joined me in the effort, like Kent Askew. Other leaders emerged from within, such as Tim Warkentin, Michael Coe, J. T. Taylor, Dave Sunde, and others. The women leaders were every bit as strong as the men. By the early 1990s, our college ministry had grown by 1000%, and we had trained hundreds of leaders in the process. I believe in the power of a spiritual leadership culture.

The Tipping Point

It's time to bring this all home. I believe a leadership culture is possible on your campus. It will simply require you to be intentional about the stuff that really matters. In his fascinating book, *The Tipping Point,* Malcolm Gladwell shares how one idea or behavior can sway the culture:

> "The tipping point is that magic moment when an idea, trend,
> or social behavior crosses a threshold, tips, and spreads like wildfire."[8]

Just as a single sick person can start an epidemic of the flu, so too can a small but precisely targeted push cause a fashion trend, the popularity of a new product, or a drop in the crime rate. I remember when fax machines were new. At first, only a few offices had them. Because they weren't yet popular, many waited to buy them. It was still easier to use the phone or to mail information because everyone had a telephone and mailbox. In 1987, however, the fax machine reached a tipping point. Enough people were using them to entice everyone else to get them. In other words, the peer pressure was positive for the fax machine. Now it's e-mail!

I believe we can create this same positive peer pressure for students to think "influence." We can help them see they can make a difference and be salt and light in their world. We must find the tipping point as we build a leadership culture. Malcolm Gladwell suggests three factors that create a tipping point:

The Law of the Few
This law teaches that only a few students are necessary if they're the right ones:
   Mavens are data banks. They influence because they're in the know.
   Connectors are social glue. They spread the message via relationships.
   Salesmen are persuaders. They convince others to be involved.

Question: *Who are the key people you should invite into the movement?*

The Stickiness Factor
This factor teaches how messages can be made to be sticky and memorable:
   The message should be transferable.
   The message should be memorable.

Question: *How can you communicate your message so that it sticks?*

The Power of Context
The power of context teaches us how ideas best travel in relationships:
   The power of intimacy
   The power of chemistry
   The power of environment

Question: *How should you format the communities to foster change?*

We can create a positive peer pressure for students to think "influence."

It's Your Turn

Let's face it. Most people who invest their lives in college students never get famous. Your name may never be in lights and folks at your high school reunion may never ask you for your autograph.

May I remind you, however, that you are not after fame. You are after legacy. Who knows where your student leaders may go, and what they might accomplish, thanks to the imprint of Christ on their life at 20 years old lived out to them through your life and commitment. Let me give you a quick quiz.

- Who taught Martin Luther his theology and inspired his work on the New Testament?
- Who visited Dwight Moody in the shoe store and spoke to him about Christ?
- What single woman equipped Bill Bright and Richard Halverson as students?
- Who was the elderly woman who prayed for Billy Graham for over 20 years?
- Who financed William Carey's ministry in India?
- Who refreshed the apostle Paul in a Roman dungeon as he wrote a letter to Timothy?
- What person helped Charles Wesley get underway as a composer of hymns?
- Who discipled George Muller and snatched him as a young man from a sinful life?[9]

Hmmm. Good questions. How did you do on your answers? Over 50 percent? Maybe 25 percent? Not quite so good? (Here's a clue—all the answers are in this book.)

Before you excuse your inability to answer the questions by calling the quiz "trivia," better stop and think. Had it not been for those unknown people, a huge chunk of church history would be missing. And a lot of lives would have been untouched. Your students need you. It's your turn to go out and leverage your influence.

Assessment

Assess your ministry culture. Is it toxic or healthy? Jot down two or three thoughts below.

If leadership were a disease, you would be a carrier. The question is, "What have your students caught from you?" What would you like for them to catch from your leadership? The space below gives you the opportunity to make a commitment to action on behalf of yourself and your students.

You are not after fame. You are after legacy.

I hope this book has been helpful for you as you evaluate your leadership abilities and skills among students and those around the university community. Hopefully this book is not the end of your leadership development. However, this book, and the others in the collegiate leadership series published by LifeWay Christian Resources are indicative of a prior leadership that has confidence in you and your ability to build new leaders. Everyone in the design group for this book and the series cannot begin to thank everyone who were positive spiritual leaders for them. It is for them, and for those yet to come, we are grateful you have taken time to share your life with us by reading the book.

Further Reading

Leaders Everywhere, Tim Elmore, Growing Leaders, *www.growingleaders.com*.
Postmodern Times, Gene Edward Veith, Crossway Books, 1994
Boomers, Xers, and Other Strangers, Rick and Kathy Hicks, Tyndale House, 1999
The Tipping Point, Malcolm Gladwell, Little, Brown & Company, 2000
Developing the Leaders Around You, John Maxwell, Thomas Nelson Publishers, 1995
Spirituality and Leadership, Alan Nelson, Navpress, 2002
Smal Group Leaders' Handbook, The Next Generation, Jimmy Long, InterVarsity Press, 1995

Endnotes

Session 1

[1]Anita Sama and Sam Ward, "College Kids Plug for Fun," *USA Today,* source: The National Center for Education Statistics, September 11, 2001, D-1.

[2]Mike Woodruff, Campus Ministry Update, *Ivy Jungle Report,* November, 2001; *www.ivyjungle.org*

[3]*Christianity Today,* March 11, 2002, 19

[4]William H. Willimon, "Reaching and Teaching the Abandoned Generation," *Christian Century,* October 20, 1993: 1016-1019.

[5]International Students, Inc. Annual Report, ISI Colorado Springs, CO., 1999.

[6]Donald G. Shockley, *Campus Ministry—the Church Beyond Itself* (Louisville, KY: Westminster/John Knox Press, 1989) 26.

[7]Alexander and Helen Astin, *Leadership Reconsidered: Engaging Higher Education in Social Change* (Battle Creek, MI: The Kellogg Foundation, 2000) 17-19.

[8]Conversation with Art Herron.

[9]Neil Howe and William Strauss, *Millennials Rising* (New York, NY: Vintage Books, 2000).

[10]Dennis Cone, ed., *Current Thoughts and Trends,* October 1998, 11.

[11]Ibid.

[12]Clarence Shedd, *Two Centuries of Student Christian Movements* (New York, NY: Association Press, 1934) 1.

[13]Samuel Sanford, *Baptist Campus Ministry at Crossroads* (Franklin, TN: Providence House Publishers, 1997) 23.

[14]Michael Gleason, *When God Walked on Campus* (Dundas, Ontario: Joshua Press, 2002) 58-59.

[15]Ibid, 77.

Session 2

[1]Bill Hybels, "The Art of Self Leadership," Leadership Journal, *Christianity Today,* Summer 2002, 86.

[2]H. B. London and Neil Wiseman, *Pastors At Risk* (Wheaton, IL: Victor Books, 1993).

[3]Daniel Goleman, *Emotional Intelligence* (New York, NY: Bantam Books, 1995) 233.

[4]Bill Hybels, "The Art of Self Leadership," Leadership Journal, *Christianity Today,* Summer 2002, 87.

[5]Truett Cathy, May 23, 2000, speaking to college leaders at "The Leadership Academy," hosted by "Growing Leaders," *www.growingleaders.com.*

[6]Ibid.

Session 4

[1]Peter Senge, *The Fifth Discipline* (CITY: Currency/Doubleday Publishers, 1994) 107.

[2]The Arbinger Institute, *Leadership and Self Deception* (San Francisco: Barrett-Koehler Publishers, 2000) 17-19.

Session 6

[1]Ethel May Baldwin and David Benson, *Henrietta Mears and How She Did It!,* Ventura, CA: Regal Books, 1966, 2.

[2]Ibid, 98-100.

[3]John C. Maxwell, *Common Threads of Uncommon Leaders,* Maximum Impact Tape, Volume 6, 1999.

[4]David Jeremiah, *The Power of Encouragement,* xxx, xxx: Vision House, 1994.

[5]Alan Nelson, *Spirituality and Leadership,* Colorado Springs, CO: Navpress, 2002, 130-132.

[6]Michael Gleason, *When God Walked on Campus,* Dundas Ontario: Joshua Press, 2002, 25.

[7]Ibid, 26

[8]Ibid, 29

Session 7

[1]Malcolm Gladwell, *The Tipping Point,* New York, NY: Back Bay Books, 2000, p. 5-7.

[2]Hugh Alexander Hopkins, *Charles Simeon of Cambridge,* London: Hodder and Stoughton, 1977

[3]Helen and Alexander Astin (UCLA), *Leadership Reconsidered: Engaging Higher Education in Social Change,* Battle Creek, MI: The W. K. Kellogg Foundation, 2000

[4]Harland Cleveland, *Nobody In Charge,* San Francisco, CA: Jossey-Bass Publishers, p. 6

[5]The Leadership Academy information can be obtained by going to: *www.growingleaders.com.*

[6]Don Madden, "The Championship Series," *Sports Illustrated,* October, 2002, pp. 50-52.

[7]Ibid, p. 52.

[8]Malcolm Gladwell, *The Tipping Point,* New York, NY: Back Bay Books, 2000.

[9]Chuck Swindoll, *Encourage Me,* Grand Rapids, MI: Zondervan Publishers, 2000.

Group Teaching Plans

A complete set of teaching plans for this book is available on the Internet. To download them, follow this path: Go to *www.life-way.com/studentministrypublishing/leveragingyourinfluence*. The teaching plans are not the final word on how this resource can be taught. The individual chapters are filled with many items that can be used by the instructor for deepening ones understanding of a chapter.

The teaching helps seek to enable you as you guide collegiate leaders though this resource. If you are a campus director or university minister leading other workers or volunteers, you will find this information helpful.

By following the same path and entering the title of the resource at the end as in "leveragingyourinfluence," you will also find the teaching plans for the other resources in this series.

Each session's teaching plan should include a time for:

Preparation

Prepare your room or meeting place.

Make sure you have enough books for each leader being trained to have a copy.

Read the session you will facilitate before you actually lead others.

Have several extra Bibles in the room so every person being trained will have a copy.

Examine the different sessions for the various elements you can use in teaching. Each bar directs you to specific information you can use in teaching, sharing, or reflecting.

Scripture references

Interactive tools for both group and personal use

The content of the session itself

Assessment

Outline for Teaching

Begin each session with prayer. This can be led by another collegiate leader or by the facilitator.

Introduce the session title and the topic for discussion this week.

Present one or more of the elements mentioned in the preparation as you begin the session.

Examine several of the items related to interactive tools for a time of commitment and clarification.

Conclude the teaching time by examining "The Assessment" section at the end of each session.

Closure

Encourage the leaders to talk with someone if they are unclear about any of the information in the session.

Give directions for what each participant is to do between now and when you meet the next time if you doing a group study. Make sure this is clear to each person.

Encourage the participants in your group to understand they leave to be spiritual leaders with students on campus.

Close your group time with pray. If this is an individual study, close your time with prayer, thanking God for His love.

A Word about
LifeWay Collegiate Ministries

Student Ministry Publishing, an arm of LifeWay Christian Resources, has been committed for over 80 years to developing collegiate leadership. With over 1000 campuses represented with Baptist Collegiate Ministry, the collegiate family is very large. Our commitment has been to minister to and help spiritually transform literally millions of students. That great tradition continues. This resource is designed to assist in equipping college leaders of leaders on campus, specifically to be equipped leaders with for college students. It is intended for those who work on the campus, in the church, and in the community with college students. It can easily be used to train Resident Advisors. It is designed for both group and individual study. As you use this resource and the others in the series, let it lead you to the other leadership resources to equip your students in developing their leadership style through experiencing:

How to Lead Without Titles
Develop Skills to Lead Others
Invest Your Life Through Mentoring

What will follow is one more book by Dr. Elmore. The fifth book in the series related to equipping the student to lead through serving. As a worker with students you have opportunities to help the Holy Spirit in the process of gifting others for leadership. Hopefully this entire series will speak to your needs and the needs of those around you on campus. Let me encourage you to share these books with a professor on your campus. Perhaps they could be part of a business ethics curriculum, or part of a class on Christian leadership. I hope you will take this challenge to your campus.

Leadership, you will discover, is best developed in a relationship that calls for spiritual accountability. At LifeWay and through the collegiate program, we still believe this is true. A spiritual strategy we use to develop collegiate leaders in churches and campus program is called CrossSeekers. CrossSeekers is a covenant-based ministry. Here are the points for spiritual accountability we feel are important to communicate to students and to live out in your life.

CrossSeekers Covenant Living
Collegians across the country are taking the pledge to seek to live in covenant relationships. Students are seeking to develop spiritually, which can be seen through the six CrossSeeker Covenant points. These are:

INTEGRITY   I will seek to be a person of integrity (2 Tim. 2:15).

WITNESS   I will seek to speak and live a relevant, authentic, and consistent witness (1 Pet. 3:15).

SPIRITUAL   I will seek to purse consistent spiritual growth (Col. 2:6-7).
GROWTH

SERVICE   I will see opportunities to serve in Christ's name (Luke 4:18-19).

PURITY   I will to honor my body as the temple of God, dedicated to a lifestyle of purity (1 Cor. 6:19-20).

CHRISTLIKE   I will seek to be godly in all things, Christlike in all relationships (Col. 3:212-14).
RELATIONSHIPS

CrossSeeker Resources
In addition to the leadership series, we also provide CrossSeeker Resources. For more information regarding these resources, you may contact the collegiate editor in Student Ministry Publishing at LifeWay (615-251-2000) or call 1-800-458-2772 for a complete listing of resources and the ability to purchase products to use with your fellow students as you seek Christ.

A Word about Growing Leaders

Growing Leaders is formerly the academic arm of EQUIP. It is a non-profit ministry committed to equipping the next generation of leaders who will impact this world for Jesus Christ. We provide adventure-learning in leadership, college leadership conferences at your campus, and video curriculum small-group resources for mentoring leaders. If you want to develop as an emerging leader, don't miss the tools we offer at Growing Leaders.

- Do you believe God has a calling on your life, but you need equipping to fulfill it?

- Do you want to impact this post-modern world, but need to gain some skills?

- Are you hungry to grow as a spiritual leader, but aren't sure where to turn?

Check out Growing Leaders. Here are a few tools we currently offer:

- **LEADERSHIP CONFERENCES**
  The Leadership Forums are a one- to two-day training events tailor-made for the needs on your campus. They can be outreach events for fraternities, RAs, student government, and more. Or they can serve to equip your present leaders in your ministry. You choose the topics from a menu. These conferences serve as a catalyst to build hunger for further personal leadership development.

- **LEADERSHIP TOOLS FOR MENTORING GROUPS**
  We also offer several tools including this resource to guide you through leadership discussions in a small, mentoring community. This series is part of what we offer. We also offer a tape kit called the "Leadership Exchange" where Dr. John C. Maxwell and Dr. Tim Elmore teach via cassette tape, then provide a workbook as you apply the principles. A third resource is the "Portrait of a Leader" series, which is a three-book series also designed for mentoring communities. Our hope is these resources will move you into a process of leadership development.

- **VIDEO CURRICULUM ON LEADERSHIP**
  Leadership Journey is designed to furnish ongoing, systematic leadership training for students. The video curriculum is divided into 72 twelve-minute segments to be viewed in class and then discussed. The segments cover the 32 Irrefutable Laws of Leadership and are taught by Dr. John C. Maxwell and Dr. Tim Elmore. We provide the videos, the workbooks, an instructor's guide, and a syllabus.

- **PERSONAL GROWTH RESOURCES**
  The Leadership Library represents dozens of books covering a variety of leadership facets, from character to vision, people skills to strategy, priorities to staff development, empowerment to courage. They are specialized in topics to allow you to zero in on the specific leadership area you want to study. You'll find tools on spiritual leadership, relationships, apologetics, prayer, vision and purpose, and more. These have been discounted for campus workers and students.

- **LEADERSHIP ACADEMY**
  The Leadership Academy is a two-week institute for students, held in the north Georgia mountains. It is designed to develop leadership qualities and skills through adventure learning, reading, interviews, field trips, mentoring groups, instruction, videos and a summer internship. It is held the last two weeks of May. For information, visit our Web site: *www.leadership-academy.org*.

- Visit us at ***www.GROWINGLEADERS.com***.

Authentic Influence: Leading without Titles

This is a collegiate leadership piece designed for those who are beginning their journey in leadership on the campus.

It is intended to be both a personal and small-group study.

It can be used in a church discipleship class or in a leadership class for college/young adults on campus.

The eight (8) chapters take the reader from why we are collegiate leaders to why we should and can be collegiate leaders.

With personal stories and a blending of Christian focus, each student can begin to see how others have developed into leaders.

Tim Elmore has a style uniquely sensitive to the needs of college students and leadership.

The first in the series.

The sessions are:

GOD NEVER CALLS A WRONG NUMBER: How God Calls a Leader

PRIMARY COLORS OF A LEADER: Four Essential Qualities We Need

BECOMING A PERSON OF INFLUENCE: How God Builds a Person into a Leader

THE FIVE LEVELS OF LEADERSHIP: Why People Follow their Leaders

STAY IN CHARACTER: The First Ingredient of Leadership

I HAVE A DREAM: Capturing a God-Given Vision

THE ART OF THE BASIN AND THE TOWEL: The Marks of a Servant Leader

YOU CAN BE A PEOPLE PERSON: Cultivating Your Relational Skills

This study is recommended for churches, campus ministry programs, and as a collegiate classroom textbook.

To order,

PHONE 1-800-458-2772

EMAIL: *customerservice@lifeway.com*

Online: *www.lifeway.com*

Wired for Influence: Skills to Leader Others

This is the second book in a series of books designed to assist college students in becoming spiritual leaders on their campuses.

It addresses needs new leaders have for the proper skills and tools to lead groups.

It is intended to be both a personal and a small-group study.

It can be used in a church discipleship class or in a leadership class for college/young adults on campus.

The eight (8) chapters take the reader from the beginning of their leadership role to how to deal with difficult people.

With personal stories and a blending of Christian focus, each student can begin to learn the skills of being a leader.

Tim Elmore has a style uniquely sensitive to the needs of college students and leadership.

The second in the series.

The sessions are:

YOUR LEADERSHIP ROLE: Precious Treasure or Performance Trap?

PRIORITIES OF A LEADER: How You Can Make the Most of Your Time

TEAMWORK MAKES THE DREAM WORK: Recruiting and Releasing Team Players

WHAT'S YOUR GAME PLAN: The Art of Strategic Planning

YOU CAN BECOME AN EFFECTIVE COMMUNICATOR: Learning to Speak the Language of Leadership

EMPOWERING OTHERS: Learning How Leaders Multiply their Results

LEADING AN EFFECTIVE MEETING: How You Can Organize and Lead a Fruitful Team Meeting

LEADING WHEN YOU'D RATHER BE LEAVING: Dealing with Difficult People and Draining Positions

This study is recommended for churches, campus ministry programs, and as a collegiate classroom textbook

To order,

PHONE 1-800-458-2772

EMAIL: *customerservice@lifeway.com*

Online: *www.lifeway.com*

Collegiate and Young Adult Interactive Leadership Bible Study

intentional influence
investing your life through mentoring

Tim Elmore
foreword by Dr. Bill Henry

Intentional Influence: Impacting Your Life Through Mentoring

This is the third book in a series of collegiate leadership books designed to assist
college students in becoming spiritual leaders on their campuses.
It addresses needs new leaders have in understanding the concept of mentoring "one-on-one".
It is intended to be both a personal and a small-group study.
It can be used in a church discipleship class or in a leadership class for college/young adults on campus.
The eight (8) chapters take the student from What is Mentoring to Deepening Your Influence.
With personal stories and a blending of Christian focus, each student can begin to learn the importance of being a mentor.
Tim Elmore has a style uniquely sensitive to the needs of college students and leadership.
The third in the series.

The sessions are:
WHAT IS MENTORING ANYWAY? Defining What a Developmental Relationship Looks Like
STARTING A MENTORING RELATIONSHIP: Who to Look For as You Seek a Paul, Barnabas, and Timothy
STYLES AND STEREOTYPES: Removing the Excuses that Keep Us from Mentoring
THE ART OF HOSTING A DISCOVERY: Learning the Nuts and Bolts of the Mentoring Meeting
HURDLES IN MENTORING RELATIONSHIPS: Remembering the Goal When Challenges Arise
GREAT GIFTS A MENTOR GIVES: Discovering the Gifts and Tools You Can Give Your Mentee
FOSTERING LIFE CHANGE: Seeing Lasting Results in People's Lives
DEEPENING YOUR INFLUENCE: Leaving a Legacy in Those You Mentor

This study is recommended for churches, campus ministry programs, and as a collegiate classroom textbook
To order,
PHONE 1-800-458-2772
EMAIL: *customerservice@lifeway.com*
Online: *www.lifeway.com*

Leveraging Your Influence

This is a collegiate leadership piece designed for those who are in leadership positions
in the church or on campus and leading students.
It is intended to be a personal study for the leader.
It can be used in the church to equip paid and volunteer leaders or in a leadership class for denominational workers.
The ten (10) chapters take the reader from Your Calling as a Leader to Developing a Leadership Culture.
With personal stories and a blending of Christian focus, each worker can begin to see how to be a leader among leaders.
Tim Elmore has a style uniquely sensitive to the needs of college students and leadership.
The fourth in the series.

The sessions are:
YOU'VE BEEN PROMOTED: The High Calling of a Collegiate Ministry Leader
TRAVELING ON THE INSIDE: The Inward Life of a Campus Minister
I LIKE YOUR STYLE: Assessing Your Leadership Identity
CHARTING YOUR COURSE: Identifying Your Vision, Planning Your Strategy
DRAWING LINES AND WRITING STORIES: Ministry Structures that Develop People
BUILDING CHAMPIONS: Recruiting and Releasing a Great Team of Volunteers
LEADERS EVERYWHERE: Creating a Leadership Culture

This study is recommended for churches, campus ministry programs, and as a collegiate classroom textbook. This book is
designed specifically for collegiate ministers, campus directors, and volunteers who work with students. It is an excellent tool,
however, for anyone desiring to develop leadership skills in ministering with college students.
To order,
PHONE 1-800-458-2772
EMAIL *customerservice@lifeway.com*
Online: *www.lifeway.com*

Additional Resources for Spiritual Leadership

Recommended by
Art Herron, Editor In Chief
Student Ministry Publishing
LifeWay Church Resources

Depending on where you are in your work and spiritual pilgrimage, these additional resources may be of service to you. Each are designed to assist you in becoming the leader in your campus program that Christ desires you to be. For your benefit they are grouped according to publishers and not by titles or authors.

The Bridger Generation: The First Comprehensive Study of the Next Generation, Thom S. Rainer, Broadman & Holman, 1997
Fresh Encounter, Henry Blackaby and Claude King, Broadman & Holman, 1997
The Leadership Lessons of Jesus: A Timeless Model for Today's Leaders, Bob Briner and Ray Pritchard, Broadman & Holman, 1997
Life in the Spirit, Robertson McQuilkin, Broadman & Holman, 2000
The Power of the Call, Henry T. Blackaby with Kerry Skinner, Broadman & Holman, 1997
The Art of Personal Evangelism: Sharing Jesus in a Changing Culture, Will McRaney, Broadman & Holman, 2003
The Young Man in the Mirror: A Rite of Passage into Manhood, Patrick Morley, Broadman & Holman, 2003

Getting on Top of Your Work, Brooks Faulkner, LifeWay Press, 1999
Jesus on Leadership, C. Gene Wilkes, LifeWay Press, 1996
Search for Significance, Robert S. McGee, LifeWay Press, 1992

Executive Influence: Impacting Your Workplace for Christ, Christopher Crane and Mike Hamel, NavPress, 2003
Friendship Counseling, Kevin D. Huggins, NavPress, 2003

Five Steps to Fasting and Prayer, Bill Bright, NewLife Publishers, 1998
Ministry of Management, Steve Douglass, Bruce Cook & Howard Hendricks, NewLife Publishers

Managing Yourself, Stephen Douglass & Al Janssen, Integrated Resources, 1978

To assist you in obtaining any one of these books, you can
     Phone 1-800-458-2772
     Internet: *www.lifeway.com*
     E-Mail: *customerservice@lifeway.com*
     In Person: Visit the LifeWay Christian Store serving you. If they don't have it, they can order it for you.